A Real Piece of Work

By day, Erin Riley is a social worker, having spent most of the last decade working alongside marginalised populations in community aged care in and around Sydney. By night, Erin's a skivvy-wearer, a dedicated reader, wrestling fan, swimmer of laps and a lover of routine. Erin brings a queer lived experience to their professional work and to their writing, and is fascinated and energised by the power of stories in both understanding and reimagining ourselves. They were a Penguin Random House Australia Write It fellow in 2021, and have been published in *Kill Your Darlings*, *Bent Street* and various corners of the internet. Erin lives in Sydney with their partner and Remy the dog.

T0352143

'Essays full of heart, soul, probing intelligence and wonderful characters.' – Fiona Kelly McGregor

'Erin Riley makes a fine companion through these stories of their life. With a knack for calm appraisal and a sharp essayist's eye, they take us through the modern world's pains and delights, its paradoxes and its people.' – Ronnie Scott

'Crisp, caring and delicate, Riley writes of turning to themselves with tenderness when at times the world can't even look or stares a little too hard. From the awakening of a young crush to the collective bricks of community, this is a nourishing read that offers up the complexity of love with two hands and a glorious moustache.' – Kaya Wilson

'What's most striking about Erin Riley's writing is its warmth – their stories are always genuine, in expression and emotion, and always huge of heart. Riley is a natural storyteller, and they combine this with a strong sense of all that's artful in the essay: there are big and important ideas within these pieces, but they're never laboured or forced. These are intimate, intelligent essays about belonging, interconnection, many and varied kinds of love, and how a person might make and find a clear calmness of self amid it all.' – Fiona Wright

A Real Piece of Work
of Work
Erin Riley

A Memoir in Essays

VIKING
an imprint of
PENGUIN BOOKS

VIKING

UK | USA | Canada | Ireland | Australia
India | New Zealand | South Africa | China

Viking is part of the Penguin Random House group of companies whose addresses can be found at
global.penguinrandomhouse.com.

Penguin
Random House
Australia

First published by Viking, 2023

'Daughters' was originally performed at Queerstories at the Giant Dwarf Theatre in Sydney (2019);
an earlier version of 'Donna' was originally published as part of Outstanding Short Story Competition (2019); 'Wrestling with Feelings' was originally published in *Kill Your Darlings* (2021); an
earlier version of 'Cat Whisperer' was originally published in *Enby Life* magazine (2020); 'COVID
Exercise Bike' was originally published in *Bent Street 5.1: Soft Borders, Hard Edges* (2021); 'The
Darlinghurst Discount' was originally published in *Queer As Fiction* (2021).

The text permissions on page 243 constitute an extension of this copyright page.

Cover design by George Saad © Penguin Random House Australia
Cover Image Have Fun All the Time By Studio Firma/Stocksy.com
Typeset in 11.5/15.45pt Adobe Garamond Pro by Midland Typesetters, Australia

Printed and bound in Australia by Griffin Press, an accredited
ISO AS/NZ 14001 Environmental Management Systems printer.

A catalogue record for this
book is available from the
National Library of Australia

NATIONAL
LIBRARY
OF AUSTRALIA

ISBN 978 1 76134 015 4

penguin.com.au

MIX
Paper | Supporting
responsible forestry
FSC® C018684

*We at Penguin Random House Australia acknowledge that Aboriginal and Torres Strait Islander
peoples are the first storytellers and Traditional Custodians of the land on which we live and work.
We honour Aboriginal and Torres Strait Islander peoples' continuous connection to Country, waters,
skies and communities. We celebrate Aboriginal and Torres Strait Islander stories, traditions
and living cultures; and we pay our respects to Elders past and present.*

For Merryn

'What you risk reveals what you value.'
– Jeanette Winterson, *Written on the Body*

'It is other people – anonymous figures glimpsed in the subway or in waiting rooms – who revive our memory and reveal our true selves through the interest, the anger or the shame they send *rippling* through us.'
– Annie Ernaux, *Exteriors*

Contents

Author's Note

The essays in this collection are reflections on my life and my understandings of the stories that have made me who I am. In the essays that speak to my work as a social worker, I have taken creative liberties, connecting the essence of many people and stories and making vague what was once specific in the interest of confidentiality and ethics. These characters are a fictionalised composite of the kinds of people I have had the pleasure to work with in the community. Elsewhere, I have changed the names of some of the other people who appear in these pages.

Prologue

Daughters

We sit in my car. You, in the black ribbed dress. The dress you modified with the scissors.

'Do I look too slutty?' you ask, turning to me, your never-nude boyfriend. My head and hands poking out from an oversized flannel.

We're going to dinner with my parents. The first time since I'd proposed to you on a dancefloor with a crumpled note summoned from my bumbag.

'You look hot.'

I'd have preferred our news to have come from us both. Instead, it was divulged during a visit when Dad began hypothesising, 'What the fuck would I say?' if his eldest daughter – me – were to ever get married.

Mum piped up, reiterating a conversation about a celebrity losing an adult son. Dad had expressed how devastated he would be to bury me. His internal rationalisation seemed to be: she may be gay, but at least she's not dead!

'Well, you might want to start thinking about that speech, Dad, because it's happening,' I croaked.

*

I'm anxious.

'I want my family to welcome you in the way yours have me – to ask you about your life.'

'I have all that I need,' you reply. You kiss me on the mouth and remind me that I am loved.

Holding hands, we close our eyes. Rain drums on the windscreen, the white noise a perfect backing track to our preparatory self-affirmations.

'Regardless of what happens, we are beautiful queer freaks making a life together,' you say.

We step out of the car. The rain has stopped, the low-hanging grey sky is split by a piercing orange orb. A rainbow shoots overhead. The gay gods, looking out for us, perhaps.

Lakemba is full to bursting. There are people everywhere, eating, spilling onto the kerb, darting in and out of cars, unloading boxes upon boxes of fresh produce from the backs of vans, stacking them atop trolleys swiftly manoeuvred into shops. We stop at a grocer that looks like the one next door, and the one next to that. We buy a mango for breakfast.

Jasmin is tucked away at the very bottom of Haldon Street; a no-frills, unflatteringly lit Lebanese joint. A treat without the trimmings. We're early.

We skim the menu.

Our backs are to the street. You flinch and I jump as Mum arrives. Mum's size matches her personality – effusive and loud. Her thoughtfulness, justice-doing and imaginings of a kinder world live in my blood, too, as does a love for a good story well told. Mum's an expert storyteller. Each story disappears into the next, a tumbleweed of words.

When I unceremoniously disclosed the engagement, Mum had found fault with my newly beloved moustache. The dusty-coloured strip of hair you'd so tenderly painted for me with the eyebrow dye you'd snuck home from the shops.

'I thought you hated the patriarchy,' she'd decried. 'Don't you want to be a woman anymore?'

At thirty-five I was finally enjoying all the permutations of my queer masculinity. I thought that Mum's understanding of this grey area in which I quite happily now lived had softened. For years, I'd been trying to be a better daughter and saw my adulthood as an opportunity to make up for all the ways I believed I'd failed as a child. As if in winning them over, the judgements might be dampened – caught in the back of the throat, swallowed and digested, never to be uttered again.

Crushed, I was too tired to explain social constructionism. My moustache was epic and Mum was oblivious to the deep joy it had unearthed. She ruminated loudly that the next logical aesthetic step was that I would surely soon tattoo my face.

Dad strolls in. He greets us with an earnest hug and a congratulatory word. He sits down opposite me. Mum is opposite you. Dad's wearing a new shirt.

Mum's adorned with a chunky necklace, a kaleidoscopic blouse, her dead sister's shoes and I notice she's wearing two of the three bands of her wedding ring (the third my sister buried in the family backyard in 1997).

The food arrives, wafts of garlic lift our spirits and our hands move fast. As happens often, there's a lot of storytelling. I fear that we will eat this dinner together but that Mum and Dad may not ask about the event that has sparked this invite.

Up until this moment, my parents have been welcoming of you in my life, even if the questions have been slow, as if written on an invisible palm card in their hands, a reminder: *Ask her a question!* The finer details of interactions and idiosyncrasies you don't see (only I notice the gaps) are made yet more striking in the context of my sister's recent engagement – a future wedding where Dad will know what to say.

An hour in, my fingers are greasy. You hold them tight at my dad's first and welcome question, 'How'd people respond to your news?' Beaming, we recount the words of beautiful, affirming friends. Your family's collective operatic screams and jumps of joy and the group hug that left me speechless. Speechless, because in my mind, *our* minds, we are play-acting. This is a play act because we didn't dream of this as a possibility for our life. Individually, we didn't dream of it for ourselves. Firstly, because it wasn't possible for queers but also, because it felt like an ideological queer crime. But we met and we loved and we wanted to have a party to celebrate this wild discovery of a lifetime. To let everyone know how fond we were of each other. That we hoped to love each other for as long as we could, ideally until we died.

Our desire to be married sat next to wanting to fuck it up, sat next to not wanting to have a baby, sat next to wanting to wear a ring, sat next to wanting to fuck someone else with it on, sat next to not wanting the only time everybody who loves us gathered in such numbers to be at our funerals.

Theatrically, Mum patted down her chest, bringing attention to the colourful top. Worn on purpose because it was the top she wore to her piano recital. The one I took you to.

'November 25,' she says. 'That's when I knew. That you were going to be together for a long time.' She had noticed how we were separate and together all at once.

My chest feels full – it's a bodily response. I look at you as if we've both shafted some magical pill. An understanding of this moment needs no words; your squeeze on my knee, the biggest yet. This is huge, the squeeze says. Look at this. You are being seen. We are being seen. I feel my chest expanding, as if creating space for this new knowledge. Mum really has seen us in a way I'd not imagined was possible. Perhaps expanding also to hold space for the guilt I felt in underestimating how far my parents could come. That their love for me could live alongside their distaste for moustaches and fades. My eyes teemed tears of joy.

Mum slides a neatly wrapped book across the table. The card she'd written mid-feast. 'No time before,' she'd said, because, 'your dad was writing his poem in there!' Opening the card, Dad's carefully crafted words are imbued with the nuances you and I felt: a thoughtful engagement with our queer life.

It was as if my parents had sensed my despair. Their very interest and curiosity was enough – but poetry?! I'm not sure what's happened but it's enough, more than enough.

It wasn't the getting married, the participation in something they understood that had hooked them, I don't think.

More that some magical penny had dropped, one jammed for years in the machine – now free, the prize finally accessible.

We peel out of the restaurant into the dark of the night. Dad, off to get the car; you on my left, squeezing my hand; Mum with her walking stick in one hand, the other interlocked with mine. She's happy, proud, even. Looking at you, Mum, projecting all her own stereotypical anxieties onto Dad, exclaims, 'You know your dad. He can deal with the Merryns and the Charlottes of the world, but you, you butcher's hook – he has more trouble with that!'

At what in the past would have had my back up, we can only laugh. It is a dream sequence, this night. The golden moment at the end of the gay rainbow. The anticipation, the steeling for disappointment – the surprises at each and every turn. Mum clambers into the car and waves us off with her stick half-in, half-out.

We stand and wave. The car drifts from the kerb. We walk, arm in arm, speechless. We pull the book, *The Thinking Woman*, from its wrapping. Mum's inscription reads:

On the special engagement event,
Dear Erin and Merryn
Our thinking women
Our daughters
Love makes the world a safer place
Love Mum and Dad

Donna

Donna. Donna with her orange hair plastered to her head in a tight plait that brushed the nape of her neck. Bright green eyes. Freckles brushed her cheeks.

I waited for Donna after each state league basketball game. Heat rising into my cheeks, colouring them a soft pink. The starting point guard for the Sydney Comets, she weaved through the game, a magician, setting up plays, nailing three-pointers like free throws. Her crossover so quick, only a double-team could silence her.

Wooden bleachers climbed the walls towards the corrugated iron roof of the ancient stadium. Fluorescent lights hung from the rafters, dangling from wobbly wiring, protected by circular silver light shades, most busted out of shape, each cratered with dents from wayward basketballs. Ads for local plumbers, real estate agents and ice-cream brands lined the walls, interrupted by scoreboards in each corner that counted down the minutes and flickered into life when points were made. A buzzer deafeningly signalled the beginning and end of play. From the top row, looking onto the court, I watched magic unfold. Basketball was like great art to me. Exquisite.

From my vantage point – aged twelve – sitting next to my dad on our BYO cushions, I watched Donna and had my breath stolen. I saw her slip by the defence and sink jump shots. I witnessed her run her opposing point guard so hard into a screen she had to be carried off the court.

At twelve, I was a prodigious basketballer and an embryonic queer. Alongside my flair for the game grew Dad's own swelling obsession. These games were our weekly education. We pulled apart the intricacies of every moment on the court. We noticed when teams moved to a full court press defence when they should have stayed in a zone to preserve precious energy, the cleverness of consistently double-teaming a point guard who was already overwhelmed.

I looked forward to Friday nights with anticipation yet unrivalled; no sleepover, no bowling-alley birthday filled my belly with such fire. Nothing came close. My state basketball zip-up jacket topped off my purposeful outfit. I wanted people to notice me. My basketball jacket was my adolescent hanky code, signalling me as a teenager with real basketball potential. I'd wear my state jacket, its NSW emblem embroidered on the right side of my chest, the rest of the jacket a configuration of white and navy and dark blue squares. I'd wear it over a pair of tracksuit pants with a crisp white pair of socks and slip-ons, as if fresh from a game myself. I'd deliberately walk to the canteen at half time, hoping to be noticed. I will be someone someday, screamed me and my crinkly, quick-dry intentional uniform. It offered me the layer of confidence

I couldn't muster without it. I'd balance a KFC box on my knees, a half-cold potato and gravy on the bench beside me. A can of Pepsi strategically opened at halftime.

Occasionally there was a junior match beforehand. Bigger versions of myself laying out a basketball life I would soon short-live. My over-the-top basketball ardour matched by gangly bodies in oversize mesh shorts in yellow, warm-up shirts emblazoned with flaming basketballs. I was flaming, too, though I didn't know it yet.

Towards the end of the first game, the state league players would stream in, sports bags heavy with gear riding on hips. All wore crisp white socks with slip-on masseur sandals. I scanned the arrivals for Donna.

I'd watch her place her bag on the players' bench, bend down to lace her high-tops. I'd watch her stand and remove six earrings from her left ear, more from her right and stow them delicately in the side pocket of the oversized bag. I'd watch her spit onto her palm, lift a sneaker to her hand. Then the other. I'd watch her step onto the freshly repolished court, spit-soaked soles squeaking her arrival. I'd watch her sink five free throws during warm-up; send the ball like a missile into the post.

The buzzer signalled the transition from aggressive shirt-pulling to sweaty hand-shaking. I waited for Donna to lug her enormous bag to the basement locker room, where on Thursday nights I would sit, sweat-drenched, ignoring the yells of a balding basketball wannabe who had no idea how to coach girls. I'd wait for Donna to emerge from her dank basement chrysalis. She'd glide across the emptying stadium towards friends in her crisp white turtleneck, taut across her breasts. Breasts so beautiful I almost lost my eyes. She wore a gold chain. Black, high-waisted jeans hugged her wide hips. Black leather boots gave her the height her sneakers couldn't.

I'd stall our departure, asking Dad to explain a play. Holding my bone-dry can of Pepsi to my mouth, I took pretend sips. Pretend swallows, too, if it came to it. Buying time to watch Donna do ordinary things in her tight, ribbed turtleneck and her chain and her hair slicked back with gel. I watched her gesture to someone she hadn't seen earlier – surprise illuminating her beautiful freckled face.

I wondered what it would feel like if she smiled at me like that. I wondered about her life away from the ancient stadium. What she ate for breakfast. I thought about her tight, white turtleneck. I thought about Donna noticing me.

When it was time to go, I watched Donna leave with her boyfriend Geoff, his left arm cupping her waist, thumb lost in her back pocket.

Obsessive-compulsive Disorder – A Short List

1. Rewriting the dictionary

It is little wonder I have a reasonable vocabulary. I owe it to the countless hours spent between the ages of twelve and fourteen rewriting the dictionary. It was not a simple task, rewriting the dictionary. It was not simply a situation of sitting next to a dictionary and painstakingly writing it out, word for word, A to Z. It was more horrifying than that. Mostly for me but also for my poor dad, who was the accidental co-author of my teenage dictionary. I look back on this experience and feel a hint of remorse for what I think now was some internalised tween misogyny on my part. I did not ask Mum to contribute much to my dictionary, despite her master's degree in education, her very bookish, politicised mind.

My obsessiveness and its compulsive shadow started showing up in my life in the form of a desperate need to know the meaning of all words. All of them. Mostly words I did not know, though it extended to 'borderline' words – words I knew the meaning of but were forgettable because they were still sort of obtuse. Basically, words that could very easily slip the mind. Words like 'malevolent', 'vindicate', 'posturing', 'innocuous', 'maladaptive'.

Somehow it came out of nowhere, my need to possess all of the meanings of all of the words. One day, words I did not know the meanings of passed by my ears and eyes constantly, effortlessly. I barely noticed them whizzing past – on the television, in books, in conversations at the dinner table. The next, nothing I did not know or understand got past me. Words clung to me as if I were a kind of adhesive teenager – I couldn't shake them off. Only writing them down and knowing their meaning provided release from their spell, which felt more like a curse as the obsession mutated into something unrelenting. Unstoppable until we found a medication that dulled it a little and I grew out of it, mostly, over the next few decades.

I would hear words on the television and write them in my notebook, immediately unable to continue watching the program until the word was transcribed, defined, understood. The home I grew up in was a converted nineteenth-century nursing home and each room was tiny. My parents' bedroom contained just their double bed. Nothing else. They would slide, side first, like crabs, into bed. The TV room was the same, and we all crammed into a sofa set like the Simpsons – two single-seaters and a two-seater couch flush against the wall. The TV had a 34-cm screen that sat in an equally small hole in the wall mere inches from our faces.

We'd be watching *The Bill* in this tiny room when PC Debbie Keane would describe some chavvy teen in a white cap who'd huffed some paint and smashed the windscreen of a beamer as a 'jocular son of a bitch' – and I'd scribble the word into my book, with its multiple pages organised A–Z with tabs. Tabs reinforced with sticky tape. Before the scene had finished, the story no longer important, I'd ask Dad for the meaning of 'jocular'. He would remind me that this book I was writing already existed. That I could simply 'Look it up'. But for me, it wasn't good enough. I needed a definition that was understood by me, in simpler terms. It needed to happen instantly and if it didn't, I was inconsolable. I would become so distressed internally, externally sometimes, too. I'd burst into tears – as if not knowing the meaning of this word right now was too much of a discomfort to bear. Later, the distress was connected to both the 'not knowing' as well as to the ways in which this obsession began to short-circuit whatever activity I happened to be engaged in. The times when I was at school, at the movies, when I overheard something juicy at the shops. Once, playing basketball I remember I heard a parent scream an obscenity I did not know. I was in the middle of a game, the ball was in play and I just walked straight off the court to the bench to write it down.

I couldn't get my head around the idea that the dictionary existed and was the easy answer to this existential linguistic distress that happened every time my ears chanced upon a new word. It interrupted so much of my life. I would stop what I was doing, pull out my notebook and write. I'd be watching some teenage rom com while eating pizza at a sleepover with my friends and some character would utter an unknown word. I'd leave the room and call home immediately on the landline. Ask for Dad.

'What's "anathema"?'

'Something or someone one hates with a passion,' came Dad's voice through the phone, as I fiercely scribbled down the experience of my OCD.

2. *Men in Black*

This was one of the first movies I was allowed to go and see by myself, unaccompanied by adults. I was dropped off by my dad at Eastgardens Shopping Centre to meet my friends Kirsty and Lisa. I had, by this point, started obsessional list-making in my head. Lists of mostly inconsequential facts or events. Sometimes it was the dishes I had eaten for each important main meal of the previous day (*cornflakes and Milo, cheese and Vegemite sandwich, two Scotch Finger biscuits, salmon patties*), while other times it might have been the main events of the last weekend, my parents' number plates, or the various buses I could catch to get to school (190, L90, L88, 188). I was also developing a terrifying fear of losing my memory, so my list-making loosely tied in with my general obsession with recounting, documenting and remembering everything possible, however mundane or insignificant. I had also come up with all the disastrous things that would happen if I were to not list things in my head (e.g. my mum would die, the house would burn down, my friends would get cancer, I would die in a horrific car accident) which made them all the more intrusive in my every day. I would repeat the lists over and over in my head, often for hours, to avoid many a catastrophe.

Cornflakes and Milo.
Cheese and Vegemite sandwich and two Scotch Finger biscuits.
Salmon patties.

Cornflakes and Milo.
Cheese and Vegemite sandwich and two Scotch Finger biscuits.
Salmon patties.

Cornflakes and Milo.
Cheese and Vegemite sandwich and two Scotch Finger biscuits.
Salmon patties.

The day I went to see *Men in Black* I took a calico library bag filled with my wallet made from quick-dry material and fastened with velcro, popular with teenagers on the Northern Beaches at the time, a party-sized bag of Maltesers, keys to the house, an extra jumper and a bottle of Pepsi.

When inside the darkness of the cinema, I took out the Maltesers and placed the Pepsi in the drink holder next to me. The aircon was freezing and so I put on the jumper while the movie trailers rolled past.

OCD is a rather strange affliction, in that it is so unpredictable and manifests in many different ways. It is surprising even to those who suffer it, from the ways our mind holds us hostage to its incredible capacity to play tricks we must overcome in order to maintain a sense of order and control or to – as it was for me – survive the day. The fight against the list-making was more painful than succumbing to the outrageous mental gymnastics that my OCD often required of me.

In the cinema I was overcome with the need to categorise the items inside my bag. Initially it was what was in the bag at the beginning of the day:

Wallet, keys, Maltesers, jumper, Pepsi.
Wallet, keys, Maltesers, jumper, Pepsi.
Wallet, keys, Maltesers, jumper, Pepsi.
Wallet, keys, Maltesers, jumper, Pepsi.
Wallet, keys, Maltesers, jumper, Pepsi.

Though once in the darkness with my jumper on, it was just the items left in the calico library bag that seemed to matter. So, all through *Men in Black* was a background noise, a low and irritating internal hum:

Wallet.
Keys.

Wallet.
Keys.

Wallet.
Keys.

Wallet.
Keys.

The list-making and -keeping occasionally became intertwined with the concern that these items may have been lost, and so often there was an action of checking that accompanied my list-making, particularly the 'what's in the bag' kind of list, as checking is quite a common accompanying compulsion. The checking doesn't work so much with lists like 'my last five meals' which, of course, are long gone.

As if my wallet and keys had magically grown themselves some legs and wandered off under the seats of all the other teenagers in the cinema watching *Men in Black* – I obsessively checked my bag for these items as I recited them in my head. I contorted myself regularly to find their familiar outline inside the calico bag resting at my feet. I'd pat the items in the dark. *Wallet. Keys.* Move back into my seat, continue my repetitive list, manoeuvre down there again. I ticced throughout the entire film. Up and down, up and down, fumbling hands in the dark: *Wallet. Keys. Wallet. Keys. Wallet. Keys. Wallet. Keys.* Up and down, up and down, fumbling hands in the dark: *Wallet. Keys. Wallet. Keys. Wallet. Keys. Wallet. Keys.* Up and down, up and down, fumbling hands in the dark: *Wallet. Keys. Wallet. Keys. Wallet. Keys. Wallet. Keys.* I cannot imagine what I looked like to my poor friends, who I know were justifiably annoyed by my continual shuffling in their periphery, though I remember the compulsion being so utterly distressing to me. But it was something I was compelled to do and I just couldn't stop. Much of my existence was often like this, filtered through a tinnitus-like internal monologue of my own deranged making, which left the outside world a little further away – as if behind a pane of glass and just beyond my reach.

The list-making has been quite the time traveller. During my late teens I was so terrorised by OCD that I couldn't fathom having a normal adult life. I was overwhelmed by the sheer exhaustion of playing by its ever-changing rules just so I could access some form of ordinary teenage existence that, at times, I wished I could just die. I never tried to hurt myself seriously but I often imagined not being alive. Feeling free of the mental anguish of being on alert all the time to banal and useless information I rationally knew was just clogging up my brain. It was that painful. So utterly intrusive – invading every space and every moment.

OCD and my compulsive list-making is something that has not been totally inescapable, though thankfully it has mellowed a lot with time – a cerebral quietening I am grateful for. Less a loud roar, more a dull thrum. One that pops up more on some occasions such as in times of stress, sleeplessness and worry. The lists are now more adult in theme. Swimming laps of the Canterbury Pool, reciting the names of the last five people I've had sex with, in order, over and over. Over and over. Wouldn't you like to know?

3. The Clock

Again and again and again until I was exhausted and fell asleep. The single bed of my childhood sat flush against the wall, wedged into the corner. My digital alarm clock with its bright red numbers illuminated the tiny wooden built-in on the opposite wall. I am, to this day, a tummy-sleeper, like a baby on tummy time who has not yet developed the strength to flip around. My nights, then and now, spent flipping my head side to side – equalising the neck-pressure such a ridiculous sleeping position engenders. My OCD clock-checking was a little bit like the bag-check situation, both in its worry that the time might have changed or disappeared (well, it does!) and also in the way it was accompanied by a strange and habitual compulsive movement.

From my spot on my tummy, in the darkness the clock was directly behind me. Sort of over my shoulder. To see it fully required I turn my head to the side and then crane it over my shoulder and lift my stomach a touch off the bed. Somehow, each night I would check the clock over one shoulder and then, as if the other had missed out, I would do the same thing on the opposite side: I'd turn my head to the other side, crane it over the opposite shoulder, lift a touch off the bed to get a proper look at the clock. Then I'd return to the middle – and then, again, this compulsion to equalise *that* movement – and so on and on it went, a relentless checking of the time and this strange, hybrid upper torso dance from side to side. Until I reached exhaustion and sleep would come. At 03:18, 12:59, 02:07.

4. Rubbish

Instead of tossing my lunch scraps in the school bins, I would collect every bit of rubbish – every banana peel, chip packet, cling wrap, cherry pip, apple core, greasy ball of crumpled alfoil, uneaten sandwich crust and empty juice container – and place them in the bottom of my bag to take home with me every day.

Much of my OCD incorporated a good dose of anthropomorphism. I had convinced myself that my rubbish was alive and had feelings of its own. That, if left in the school bins, it would be lonely, cold and scared. It would feel discarded and unloved – especially so in the night-time, when the school-yard was a ghost town. I was so pained by the thought of my rubbish being 'left' in the bins that for over a year I brought it all home. Sometimes I would squash it all back inside my lunchbox; at other times, without a container to hold it, it would just loosely float around in my schoolbag's increasingly compost-y interior. I'd get home and sneak outside to dump the day's contents into the large council bin we kept outside in the yard.

This eventually became a ritual. I found a way to contain the distress at the thought of 'abandoning' the rubbish by simply taking it home where I had convinced myself it would be better tended to in a different but proximal bin. There were a few odd moments where, on some of the harder days, I would extend this distress to the rubbish of others or the rubbish already in the school bin, or headed for it. I would collect, hoarder-like, the additional rubbish of my friends (casually I'd say, 'Oh I'll take that to the bin for you,' before disappearing around a corner only to shove it expertly into my bag), even dive into bins, to 'save' a thing or two, if I could guarantee I wouldn't be seen. These items would end up in the bin at home – destined for a better life.

Wrestling with Feelings

hardcorelegend_3in1@hotmail.com was my first email address. It was my wrestling-obsessed thirteen-year-old self's nod to the World Wrestling Federation's Mick Foley and his three alter egos: Mankind, Cactus Jack and Dude Love.

As a young person, I lived two lives. Outside of school I dreamed of making basketball a career. I played multiple times a week, shooting free throws late into the night. On weekends I mopped up the sweat of the mid-90s premier women's basketball team, the Sydney Flames, who drew crowds of up to 6000 at the Sydney Entertainment Centre. After the game, I watched the players, in their civilian clothes, be waited on by fans and friends by the bar. It was my first glimpse of queers – women in high-waisted blue jeans and black leather jackets. Some had peroxided hair gelled back and held the hands of hot femmes. My nebulous queer identity was finding its form.

When I wasn't playing basketball, I was watching or thinking about wrestling. I was reading ghostwritten wrestling autobiographies and ordering magazines in the post. I was spending evenings at the local library on one of two computers that had the internet. I paid ten cents a page to print wrestling stories from the web, sputtered out line by line from the inkjet under the librarian's desk. My bedroom walls were lined with posters: Chyna, 'Stone Cold' Steve Austin, Brett 'The Hitman' Hart.

Back in the 90s, wrestling was not a readily available indulgence. You watched it on cable TV or you hired the latest pay-per-view WWF Main Event, three months out of date, from the New Releases section of the video store. My favourite thing, age thirteen, was to sit cross-legged on the threadbare blue-grey carpet of Video Ezy, lost in VHS wrestling covers.

My other life was spent at Narrabeen Sports High School being bullied relentlessly. Year 10 girls hovered in the toilet doorway shouting 'This is the GIRLS' toilet!' and 'DYKE!'. Once, one pushed me over when I tried to sneak in under their arms.

'What's a dyke?' I asked Mum through tears. Surreptitiously, she'd been attending the local PFLAG group for years and had been trying to convince my dad to come along, too. Having an undercut in 1997 was apparently a gay giveaway.

I later learnt I was in fact a dyke, and later still, that I was a faggot, too – traipsing a transness I had no language for.

Mum recounted the story of telling Dad my coming out news. She said he blamed himself, making a connection between my sexuality and my penchant for sport. Basketball. Too much quick dry. WNBL lesbians. And somehow, wrestling, too. All those gay enablers.

*

There are things that we do to settle the nervous system. We meditate, go for a swim, phone a friend. Wrestling served as a way to regulate a nervous system assailed by bullies and confused about gender and sexuality. For me, wrestling had a format that was knowable, and therefore a comfort. Like *MasterChef*, like *Married at First Sight*, like *Survivor*. Predictable and safe. Cosy, easy and warm.

I don't know if Dad believed the theory that wrestling 'made me gay', as we've never spoken about it. I imagine it was hard as a parent in the 90s not to be influenced by the insidious and overt machismo of the times. To hold some warped belief that only people who failed at parenting ended up with gay kids – because being gay was somehow failing at life. I didn't know what to make of the idea that indulging in slightly masculine activities, activities that 'boys' enjoy, impacted on the carving out of one's sexuality. These loose connections speak more to the ways we internalise social myths and how gender has been constructed, and play to the binaries strengthened by language and the norms of everyday life. Of course, it is misguided, but I can piece together the reasoning.

And wrestling was *so* gay.

There was Goldust, who minced towards the ring in a shoulder-length white wig, ceremoniously wrapped in a fluffy floor-length golden robe. His theme song played as glitter dripped from the ceiling. Once in the ring, he'd pull, slowly, the golden gloves from each hand, drop the robe to reveal a glittering golden head-to-toe, full-body leotard. At the time, I thought Goldust was trans, or at least lived a life in the middle. His character often caught so much flack for being 'weird', and subtle transphobia peppered announcers' descriptions of him as 'bizarre' and 'an absolute freak'. Under the wig, his head and face were painted black and incandescent gold. Black lipstick. Black eyeliner.

There was 'Macho Man' Randy Savage, who wore leopard print tanks three sizes too small, sometimes with his midriff showing.

There was The Ultimate Warrior. Streamers ringed his steroidal biceps and his boots, pink and green and blue. He'd slip under the bottom rope, rise and pull the top one, using it to steady himself, gyrating his hips back and forth towards the sky.

The announcers, JR and Jerry 'The King' Lawler, joked and gesticulated. Lawler, an ex-wrestler himself, wore a crown and robe, open at the front to expose his naked, rosy chest; JR, never without his cowboy hat or signature Texan drawl. They were favourites, too, threading into match commentary storylines we'd forgotten, priming audiences for the next event.

Looking back, even Hulk Hogan was quite gay. His blond hair and his manicured porny blond moustache. His yellow tank top with its purposely holey back – perfect for when he reached the ring and slowly ripped it in half to uncover, bit by bit, his chiselled, hairless pecs.

The Royal Rumble is a thirty-wrestler melee, one of the WWF (now WWE)'s tentpole annual events. Each wrestler comes out at timed intervals. Initially one is in the ring and then another runs out, then another – until it is mayhem. The winner is the last one standing.

In 1998's Royal Rumble, all three of Mick Foley's alter egos brawled, albeit at perfectly timed intervals. Cactus Jack, Foley's most bloodthirsty alter ego, and also known as 'the world's most dangerous wrestler', was the first to enter the ring. Cactus Jack, in his signature outfit of a shirt emblazoned with his own 'Wanted: Dead or Alive' poster, was infamous for his ability to withstand pain and inflict brutality. He'd mastered his craft in Japan's hardcore scene, taking part in Japanese Death Matches, some of which involved barbed-wire ring ropes, or thumbtacks dusting the ring onto which Jack would back-slam opponents into bloody submission.

After one competitor had been tossed into the audience, another would appear, minutes later, to tear down the entrance and dive under the bottom rope. Mankind was the most successful of Foley's alter egos. He was a chubby, hairy creature who wore a Hannibal Lecter-esque leather mask. A crazed loner from an asylum. He suffocated his opponents with his signature move, the mandible claw – a manoeuvre in which he pulled a sock puppet (Mr Socko) out of his tight brown leggings and choked his challenger until they passed out.

After a third sweaty costume change, the last to enter was Dude Love, a tie-dyed, reflective-spectacled bohemian from the 70s.

The magical thing about wrestling is the suspension of disbelief. Wrestling and its fans, complicit in a dance of suspended reality, willingly indulge in and maintain a space of make-believe.

We knew Dude Love, Cactus Jack, Mankind and Mick Foley could never face off in a match, be anywhere at the same time. We believed it because we wished it to be real.

In my twenties, I had my own gay identity crisis. Was I a lesbian or was I a gay man? At the time, I'd returned to wrestling, rewatching old matches on my laptop. I was curious about a life in the middle. What I felt was a constant ebbing and flowing across gender.

Wrestling fostered in me deep curiosity about bodies, gender and sexuality. An idea of being many things simultaneously. The posters on my walls depicted the kinds of people I found attractive. They were the bodies I desired and desired to have myself. I loved wrestling because it demonstrated the largesse of what identity could be, especially as a genderqueer person who had few cultural reference points.

For a long time, I denied myself the space to acknowledge that I might be trans. It took me years to openly acknowledge the changes I had long desired for my own body. Only recently, while in the middle of writing this essay, my therapist asked me how I felt, physically, about my transition. She says I tend to talk myself out of things I desire that might afford me a more comfortable sense of self. She sees me scuffing my shoes on the 'rug of tolerance', shovelling things under there, which means I live some kind of self-effacing half-life.

I spoke for the first time to her about thinking about not having breasts anymore. I wanted to look like the wrestlers in my childhood posters, I told her. To fit into a white ribbed singlet without the need to bind tight with elastic. For a small amount of hair to sit, neatly, above my top lip. Maybe a small tuft of chest hair, inching towards the banner tattoo that sits along my clavicle that reads *wrestling with feelings* and is book-ended by images of embracing wrestlers.

Up until recently I had not voiced these desires aloud to anyone. I have told the people I love the most that I don't mind having breasts. *They are tiny anyway. They can be hidden.* I worry that those I love, with whom I have the pleasure of enjoying them, will be sad about their absence, if that is what I choose.

I have been fortunate to live among queer family in which there is a culture of affirming one another. In this world, not unlike that of wrestling, we embrace the expansion of belief, a world of multiple realities. Queers make their own stories, defy norms, live lives permanently in the middle.

Mankind, Cactus Jack, Dude Love – they were all parts of Mick Foley. I drifted to these wrestlers because I too was many things at once, and wished to be understood as such. The suspension of disbelief that came from Foley's adoring fans upon his entry into the ring no matter which incarnation of himself – I wanted that for me. For people to acknowledge the various ways in which I knew myself. People shouted and cheered for each version of Mick Foley and each sat, neatly and acceptably alongside one another. He was, for me, the first model of the possibility of the multiplicity of identity. I am grateful for wrestling – and, yeah, for how it made me gay.

Mum and the Piano Teacher

When I was shortlisted for the fellowship that turned into the book you are reading now, I texted my mum. She didn't reply for a day or so.

> Mum, did you get my text?

I was busy on the spin bike when she called back, leaving her usual, two-minute voicemail monologue. Reminding me, as always, several times, who she was:

Erin, it's Mum.
Sorry love, it's me, Mum, I should have responded sooner, lovey. Speak with you soon. It's Mum here, love, speak later. Mum.

Sometimes she even worked into her voicemails, both her title, in relation to me (my mother) and her actual name, Antoinette, as if I needed more help.

Mum had been in Canberra with her friend Jessie at the Botticelli to Van Gogh exhibition at the National Gallery.

Mum shot me a text, a photo of her next to Van Gogh's *Sunflowers*, all smiles. The yellow, she tells me when I next visit, was 'luminescent', as if backlit by the sun.

I love that my mum, who is seventy-two, has a best friend who is her thirty-year-old piano teacher. Jessie drove them to Van Gogh in her new Mercedes. Jessie had gifted Mum the tickets for her birthday. She had scoffed at the idea of staying in a motel and booked a lush, serviced apartment with one king-sized bed. I imagined my mum, strapping on her CPAP machine, struggling into the bed, with Jessie cocooned in a plush hotel doona on the other side. Them laughing together into the night.

I wrote to *Good Weekend* magazine during the first wave of COVID in 2020, suggesting Mum and Jessie for their popular 'Two of Us' profile. My mum, this outspoken white, fat, retired nurse with a heart of gold, and her Chinese piano teacher, whose wealthy family constantly bribe her to get married.

The editor wrote back; they had too many (ha!) 'Two of Us'-es. And so, the story is mine to tell.

Mum and Jessie have season tickets to the Sydney Symphony Orchestra. Pre-COVID, Mum had, at the classical music radio station she volunteered for, 'won' a yearlong subscription at their silent auction – which she had in turn gifted Jessie. I later found out her bid was a generous twice the going rate. My dad drives them into the heart of the Opera House car park and drops them next to the lifts.

In the early days of their friendship, Jessie was learning to drive. Before the Mercedes, she learnt to drive in my mum's

Smart Car. She would chauffeur them around to classical music concerts in obscure suburban community halls. To see the seventy-nine-year-old Argentinian concert pianist Martha Argerich play the Concert Hall. Sometimes Mum paid for piano lessons in driving time.

Jessie and Mum do a lot of texting. It's long since gone beyond co-ordinating the next piano class. Mum, one for long, novelesque messages, now sometimes flicks off an emoji. I know this is Jessie's influence. A wilted rose, followed by a correction – one standing up – then a text-based rationale for the original emoji misdemeanour. Jessie fixed Mum's GPS and taught her how to talk on the phone using Bluetooth in the car. Mum can send photos and now forwards on photos of my niece and nephews coupled with a short history of noticeable developmental milestones.

Last week, in preparation for the arrival of my parents' new couch, Mum texted me, asking whether I might post the old couch on a closed Facebook group I am a member of. 'Sure,' I replied. She sent through two blurry photographs of the couch, which had been covered in a recently washed but still hideous linen overlay adorned in brown swirls. I asked her for a few better shots and some measurements. That she sent though, reluctantly, with a reminder, 'Remember Erin, it's Facebook, not *Vogue*!'

Jessie has been in Mum's life for a few years now and has become a part of our family. I will visit my parents and Jessie will be there having a cup of tea. My dad's a teacher, and often I'll see them at the kitchen table, noses glued to Jessie's laptop, workshopping edits of an essay draft. I know Dad is thrilled to be of help. He had long been let go as guest editor by me and my sister, now a school teacher herself. Jessie has brought something so beautiful to both my parents.

One time I visited them and found a fluffy ginger cat scurrying around the unit.

'Who's that?' I asked.

'Oh, that's Brahms!' quipped Mum.

Jessie had gone away for the weekend and my parents were happily cat sitting. For almost twenty years, they had two cats of their own, both dying within a year of each other. One of them spectacularly so, between the top of the couch where he was sleeping one night and the cushion onto which he fell dead between my parents while they were watching reruns of *The Bill*.

To stay working and living in Australia, Jessie is required to always be studying. Her parents' money is helpful, though she is relentlessly bombarded with threats and bribes to come home. She's almost thirty and they can't see why she'd want to teach when her family leave her wealthy enough to do nothing. In between teaching six to ten piano prodigies a day, ranging in age from six to seventy-two (Antoinette, my mum, Antoinette, proudly claims to be Jessie's oldest student), Jessie has finished a Bachelor of Music. She has learnt to be a Mandarin–Australian translator and now she's onto a Masters of Education.

If Jessie's not around, Mum and Dad will give me the latest update. 'Erin, guess what happened to Jessie today?!' they'll offer as I plop down in their cluttered dining room. They'll tell me about how they were able to explain some obscure

Australianisms to her, express their distress at her experience of COVID-related racism.

As an adult I have moved further away from my parents. Not geographically; I'm still just three suburbs away. Emotionally though, I have a greater distance to travel now. For a long time, I didn't feel accepted as a queer person by my parents and sensed they were ashamed of my masculinity, how I inhabited gender. I held ideas that if I was a 'good enough' child, I'd earn the love and acceptance I needed and wanted. I spent a lot of time trying to prove my worth. Making parts of myself smaller, inconsequential. I showed up and listened to my mother's problems and worries in a way that as a therapist, I now know lacked boundaries.

My parents struggled, I think, with my identity, first out of a worry that life might be harder for me. For them, like many boomers, shaking the narratives that shaped the Catholic culture of their own upbringing was a task in and of itself; one I could see them continually reckon with. Their love was always there, I know this deeply now. I had no time, then, for their difficulty understanding me, and I didn't give them a lot of room to have their struggles.

I wasn't curious about where their lack of comprehension came from, or what might have been happening for them. I couldn't consider at the time that they might have been doing the very best they could. I was dogmatic and reactive, hard and cutting.

My sister is Jessie's age, thirty. For a number of years, during my sister's late teens, my parents separated. I had already moved out, started haunting queer venues, found a ratty share house. My sister was volatile towards our parents, mostly verbally, but she was most spiteful towards our mum. Mum moved out. She left first to live in an over-55s community housing co-operative full of independent geriatrics. Later she skipped the state altogether and relocated to Tasmania to run the Older Person's Unit at the Royal Hobart Hospital. I saw Dad siding with my sister and felt angry, as it signalled to me that the spiteful behaviour was permissible and that Mum didn't matter.

I probably should not have done this, but, in an attempt to understand family patterns, I once wrote a 3000-word paper about my family for my Masters. I received my first high distinction. My own upbringing provided so many examples of systems gone awry, triangulation and confused family hierarchies. It was a dream case to review, albeit for a long time, a very difficult family to exist within. It was a no-brainer, to embellish that I'd met this family of four, de-identified of course, in my hospital emergency department, after the younger sister had plunged her arm through a window following an argument.

I studied how systems theory challenged the long-held pathologising psychological frameworks that came before and viewed families as existing within a network of interweaving generational family patterns, influenced by the larger social and cultural systems they occupy. It contends that problems aren't just within the individual, but constructed socially, and encompass all the intersectional edges they touch: culture, race, gender, class etc.

Jay Haley, an early theorist of family therapy and one of the founding figures of the psychotherapy movement, noted that humans have a fundamental compulsion to organise and that organisation within family systems is important. Patterns between members of families usually operate according to hierarchies, and they tend to work according to hierarchical 'rules' (i.e. parents are the caretakers of kids), and it's when these are broken that the system becomes 'confused'. And so, for a long time, my family was confused.

It was devastating. I wanted to see them as a team, my dad as Mum's ally in the midst of verbal assault. There was a hierarchical rupture in the family structure, Mum moved out and my sister, Electra-like, swooped in to replace her.

To me, I saw Dad choosing my sister over his wife. I often went into battle for her, was angry on her behalf. I overstepped the boundaries, taking on battles that were not mine. Back then our family was split into two opposing teams.

Another aspect of systemic work is that of triangular processes. It's the notion that most pairs are inherently unstable due to people's differing needs for either closeness or distance and recruit a third to stabilise them. I used to do it all the time in my relationships whenever I sensed the distance of an avoidant lover. I'd text my best friends screenshots of my relationship drama, recruit them to my side, desperate to be soothed.

My family was triangulating all over the place. There were coalitions forming and we'd gang up against one another. Dad and my sister versus me and Mum. When coalitions occur across levels of a hierarchy – basically when parents don't stick together – that's when you know the organisation's in trouble.

I read over my old essay recently, and while it was useful in understanding patterns better, it was still only a map of the territory of my family. Indeed, I had also conveniently written out my own role in the family games. Written from a distance, as if my fictional character were someone else, my own compulsion revealed itself as that of organiser. I'd positioned myself as some kind of expert on what was going on, diluting my own role in how the dynamics played out. My own point of the triangle was somehow less pointy.

I was convinced that I knew, objectively, what was going on. It was true that I had read my 'fake' family quite well in the assignment – given that hypothesising is part of the work. But I was living there. Inside it. People's inner worlds, perceptions, motivations and experiences are never fully understood. My assumptions about my family, their experiences and what they thought (of me, about the world etc.) had got in the way of making room for alternative narratives. I wasn't so much curious as I was rewriting a story.

Mum eventually returned from Hobart. She lived with her sister for a bit, my parents got back together and they decided to sell the family home.

Just before Sydney found itself in lockdown again in July 2021, my parents took my partner and me out to dinner to celebrate the writing fellowship I'd been awarded. As my mum sat down, I noticed a whopping bruise above her left eye. A shiny purple-y thing, slowly turning a soft mauve. Some two weeks before, she'd fallen over after catching the bus to the city for a refugee rally, tripping on uneven pavement. She'd smashed her head on the ground and slashed one of her fingers to the bone, right there on Bridge Street in the middle of the CBD. Supported by beautiful strangers, Mum laughed and joked with them, who, before the ambulance arrived, bandaged her head as if she had been wounded on a battlefield.

Did she wish to call anyone?

No thanks.

Mum was taken to St Vincent's, had a brain scan, her hand stitched and when discharged, called my dad, calmly from the cafeteria, asking if he'd pick her up. She'd just decided to visit another Sydney hospital, she told him.

That was my mother's fourth fall that I know of, in the last year. The second to land her in a large tertiary Sydney hospital. The fall before that she had after Christmas at my sister's place and was equally serious. She'd dislocated her new-ish hip and needed two ambulance crews and a tarpaulin to retrieve her from her position on the floor, immobilised by pain she recalled was worse than childbirth. Her first hip replacement she had acquiesced to only after years of grinding bone-on-bone pain. She has a high pain threshold, my mum. She takes after her mother, my nanna, for whom it was a rare event to resort to a few Panadol. The doctor was shocked Mum was even still walking.

I felt a sense of outrage that she hadn't told me about the latest fall. I had texted about my own health scare the week before and she was characteristically warm and beautiful. While I didn't want breast cancer, I was also contemplating the darker but positive flip side of free top surgery courtesy of Medicare. Imagining my mum in her predicament, vulnerable in such a public way and unable to reach out for support, was distressing. I felt the sadness physically in my chest.

Antoinette, like me, is a rescuer; we support others and often dismiss our own needs. I see a lot of my own traits in her and perhaps it's why I tend to project my stories onto her. That said, she does tell me what her stories are – that she is a 'waiter', she 'puts up' with things, she has a 'role'. I keep trying to understand why Mum keeps living by these rules and it is hard to extricate myself to a place of just accepting this is how things are. She didn't call me after the fall. That was the choice she made. I watch her so often denying herself the things she deserves, the care and support we have endless capacity for.

Once I went to the US on a three-week holiday and came home to the news that Mum had not only had a cancer diagnosis but also lightning-quick surgery in the time I was away. She didn't want to spoil my holiday, she told me on the way home from the airport. I wonder if her telling those who love her in moments of vulnerability means that her vulnerability is seen, and so becomes real.

Mum was an aged care specialist nurse. She managed nursing homes and entire hospital geriatric wards. She devised tasks for patients most 'disruptive' on the ward, avoiding the need for chemical restraint so often used in hospital settings. I would visit her office as a teen, often to find an older patient who believed themselves to be at work busily filing blank pages into manila folders, muttering into Mum's unplugged extra phone, endlessly feeding the paper shredder. Cradling the ward's fake baby.

I am watching as my mum is becoming, has become, the person with the kinds of vulnerabilities she once provided support, care and specialist guidance to. It is complicated, too, for me, as someone who has worked in community aged care, sometimes case managing for periods of months and years, older people with whom I fostered rich connections. Older people whose decline in the community I witnessed. I placed a number of previously independently living people into nursing homes after catastrophic falls.

At the dinner with the bruised eye, we talked about the semantics of 'falls'. There is a shift, from 'someone fell' to 'someone had a fall'. Falls are no longer the accidental misstep of the mostly well and sprightly – as in 'he fell over at the footy'. Whoops. 'Having a fall' implies some kind of weakness, it conjures up ageing and disabled bodies. The fall has happened to you. There is a moment in time after which you become someone who has 'falls'. A metric used to assess your risk and safety at home. They are nevertheless a real thing and falls take on different meanings across the lifespan. They are one of the biggest killers of older people and the leading cause of injury-related deaths in Australia, where 37 per cent of them are from falls.

Thus, I am beginning to see the reversal of family roles. I have reached the period of my life that signals big losses are coming, they might happen soon. I am angry, too, owing to my fear of loss. There are ways I think Mum can live differently, that can facilitate a safer way of doing the activities she most enjoys. In my mind, attending to her own health issues when they pop up and caring for herself might allow her to live longer, and be the difference between a prolonged independence and heartbreaking decline. It is harder to see this in family than in the patients I was supporting. There is more to lose, for she is my mother. And so it remains such a challenge to take an accepting back seat – which, really, is where I know I should live with my mouth shut. Though this is a tough ask in a Smart Car where there aren't any back seats. I would like to see Mum hailing a cab while so unsteady on her feet. She scoffs when I encourage this and has never indulged such 'luxury'. It is not monetary luxury she is talking about, for my parents are comfortably middle class, but a personal one.

Harriet Lerner, the respected American psychologist who writes about women, discusses the ways in which mothers are either glorified or blamed in society. She notes that the role and rules of motherhood are unreachable for women and that mother-blame has been deliberately constructed within patriarchal society. Lerner reminds us that 'nowhere is the personal so political as in the mother–daughter relationship' and that adult daughters have a rough time freeing themselves from the lens that has constructed mothers this way. Daughters are so often disappointed in them without really knowing their mother's own history and wounding.

In some ways, Mum hasn't had a traditional type of mother–daughter relationship with either me or my sister (not that I consider myself a 'daughter'. As a non-binary person I'm not sure what I am, for I am not her son, either). While we are close, our closeness is now less entangled. In my distress at what was happening within her marriage and upset with Dad on her behalf, I took on the role of confidant and played the support so I didn't need to share my complicated inner world, for fear of disappointing her. Her relationship with my sister – from my perspective – was removed, cold and one-way. I saw my mother reach for closeness often, only to be rebuffed. I have watched on as this relationship has softened now that my sister is a mother as well. As Grandma, Mum has found new ways to support her daughter.

Lerner, I discovered, also had a triangulated relationship with her parents. Much like Mum, Lerner's mother would confide in Lerner all the things she found difficult about her father; all the ways in which she felt failed by him. For Lerner, this obstructed an independent relationship with each parent. Carrying the intimate information she wasn't meant to have obscured how she perceived her father for a long time. And so, even for those most alert to the systems at play in families, it remains a struggle to do the family untangling.

Mum's relationship with Jessie has given her another opportunity at mothering, sort of. However, this time, each has been chosen by the other. Jessie is there, deep in their friendship, by choice. She continues to show up. She has chosen Mum and continues to choose her, and, by extension, Jessie has chosen our family. As the years roll on, Jessie has established her own unique and independent relationship with my parents. She is the third point of a triangle, one that has come in and so beautifully stabilised their relationship.

I feel pride and love swell in my chest when I think about this relationship that crosses generation and culture. I am filled with gratitude seeing Mum so happy in her friend's company. It has helped me feel less guilty about the ways in which I have consciously stepped back and learnt to develop better boundaries. There is nothing to be guilty for, I know this, and the dynamic feels so different now. It is what a healthy relationship with a parent looks and feels like and I am slowly adjusting to its fit. I watch on as Mum supports Jessie's bids for autonomy from *her* family, her resistance to the norms of Chinese culture, and her own complicated relationship with family. Antoinette is like a progressive fairy godmother and I can see so clearly her values from my space on the sidelines cheering on. They are anti-capitalist and radical. I can see the values and politics she holds so close are the ones that motivate her to catch buses and demand justice for asylum seekers and an end to indeterminate detention. The politics that take her to peace meetings and see her personify the military–industrial complex, an ostentatious crown on her head, in a piece of radical street theatre at Central Station. The politics that, at age twenty-seven, early in her psychiatric nursing career, saw her house and care for her psychotic brother in my parents' flat, managing his medication, keeping him alive and out of hospital.

These were the values and politics I missed when I was younger, too busy with my own story. I know Mum has trouble with my gender expression, my queerness. Her difficulty obvious in small and often very brief moments. Her words were painful to hear but I can see now, she is learning to unlearn. She would align masculinity with unattractiveness in women, express a disappointment in the shortness of a new haircut. I blamed it on ignorance, labelled it homophobic, yet ignored everything that had shaped and crafted these myths about how women must be and how easy it is to get caught in cultural traps.

I held so tightly to these moments of maternal disaffection and it became the only story. It is psychologically proven that humans very easily register and remember the bad. Negativity bias, it's called – and it means we often don't notice all the good stuff – so prone we are to sitting with slights. I glossed over so many of the positive moments. I saw but didn't properly appreciate her interest, her superhuman memory for important events and dates and people in my life, her generous financial support, her thoughtfulness, her humour. Lerner says we hold 'stories', not only our own, but about our mothers, too. That we often don't want these stories to be interrupted. Because interrupting them might lead us to a painful clue about our own.

My own tightly held idea that Mum was only disappointed in me shaped a belief of not being worthy, not being good enough, that queer must be bad. I slunk into spirals of shame. I didn't curiously enter into any conversations to check anything else out, discover what else my mum was thinking, or what had shaped her worry for me. I participated in what Lerner coined a kind of 'de-selfing' – whereby I silenced the parts of myself I thought challenged the relationship and held onto my own story of who Mum was. It was my story of her story. It allowed me to blame her without much curiosity as to how I had also participated in my own self-diminishment and how the story limited us really seeing each other.

The story that I wasn't understood, was somehow less loveable, was, while protective, also the only story I had – and it led me, to a degree, to hide and keep things at a distance – so afraid of disappointing her. I realise now, in watching Mum's solidarity with Jessie, in their rich friendship, in the values that shape it, just how much capacity she has to love. And it is maybe this reason, why now, I am so desperate for more years in which Mum is here, vibrantly alive.

Cat Whisperer

One of the most beautiful displays of love I've had the pleasure of witnessing is between an ancient man and a cat.

I often see his contorted frame buckling under the weight of two green shopping bags. Each one always neatly square and full, perfectly balanced and tightly held in his strong, ageing hands. He carries a backpack, too, and wears a navy hat that covers his weathered face. Wisps of grey hair creep out from its edges. He walks at a pace that belies his age (he is, at the very least, eighty-five) and the weight of his bags. I have seen him in Marrickville, in Enmore, in Stanmore and as far as Camperdown. Sometimes when driving home from work I would see him marching steadily up Salisbury Road with his neat and boxy treasures.

I used to see him a lot more because, back then, he used to perform his act of love daily, right under my bedroom window. My bedroom window, in the red-brick corner block by the pool where I no longer live. He wouldn't know me, but I watched him most evenings immersed in his daily ritual as the purples and oranges of dusk rolled into the park. A ritual I now know was just one of many.

Before it became my bedroom window, I used to swim most nights at the pool across from it. Leaving the pool, I would look up at the red-brick corner block – its long windows like eyes. A dull pink illuminating the room of someone I didn't know. I would gaze up into its soft face when I climbed into my car. I would say to myself: *one day I'll live there*. My fantasy second home by the pool.

Under the bedroom window that eventually became mine, there was a small verge – a patch of green between the footpath and the road barely enough to even be considered a verge. Verging on verge. There was a tree on the verge and under that tree used to live a mostly white and brown, mangy stray cat. She was lovely. She had sharp edges, wild eyes and a decrepit, furry body, all clotted and slightly grubby. Day in, day out, she lived happily in the shade of the verge-tree like a queen.

Every dusk, I would watch the man cross the street, the pool mostly emptied of people as the sun faded, to feed his mangy queen. He would place his bags by his sides onto the grass.

Without his bags his body curved as if it were still carrying them. He would pat his angel softly and with a ninety-degree tilt from the hips. He'd slide his backpack off, dropping it at his feet and out of it pull a hairbrush, which he'd use to lovingly and slowly massage her back. I had tried many times to pat the mangy cat. I consider myself to be 'good with cats' – slow, patient and crouch-y – but this cat would have none of it. She wouldn't let herself be patted by anybody but him.

My partner, whose bedroom it was before it was also mine, said this daily ritual we were witnessing was one of the most beautiful acts of love they'd ever seen. We would watch the man's devotion from the window, our eyes brimming with tears. A cat has never been so loved.

From his green bags he would remove many Tupperware containers. He'd line them up and the cat would sit patiently, watching. Each was filled with assortments of wet and dry food. Then he'd take out a series of small bowls from his backpack and place them side by side. A cat buffet. He'd fill one of the bowls with water from a plastic bottle. Once he poured her some milk as a treat.

The cat would rise and devour her three courses while the man stood and watched or, sometimes, she allowed him to continue softly brushing her as she ate. After ten minutes, the man would methodically pack up the tubs of food and place them back inside the green bags. He'd rinse the bowls with the water, place them in a plastic bag, tie it, and then put it all back into his backpack. Then he'd slowly manoeuvre it in a sort of slow, curved toss onto his back from one side. I could tell he had done this many times, refining his technique. His flat back caught the bag every time. He would weave his arm through the bag's other strap, pat the cat one last time, and from his waist, bend to retrieve his green bags.

As it edged towards winter, we noticed that the cat had acquired a small tent. We would often see her grotty face poking out from inside. There were even a few blankets inside it. The man, slowly and over many days, had constructed her a shelter from the rain.

It was usually dark by the time he left. His shuffling, symmetrical silhouette would turn back towards the park – a marker of the day's end. I wondered how many local strays got this regal treatment. His bags were clearly so heavy and I imagined there must be other strays he kept good care of. I imagined him walking the streets for hours, following a methodical and timed-to-the-minute route. A band of stray cats waiting for their favourite person to arrive. I wondered whether our mangy verge friend was the last on his rounds. Perhaps his favourite. From my vantage point, I couldn't imagine anyone could love more wholesomely.

I came home one day to horrifying news. 'Something awful has happened,' my partner told me as I came through the door. A few days before, some well-meaning people from the cat protection society dropped by, asking after the scruffy creature we had become very fond of. It was a stray but a loved, well-fed and very happy stray, they informed them.

Despite being assured of her fine street life, the well-meaners returned to remove her. Our scrappy queen scaled a tree and two fire engines arrived. They tried to catch her in a net. Put the hose on her. She jumped down, escaped the net and ran away.

The elderly man came as usual that dusk to feed his favourite but she wasn't there. We watched him from the window – checking her little house, looking up and down the street. We waited, too, for our verge neighbour to return. For days we hoped to see her back, propped in her spot under the tree. But she never returned. We watched her home disintegrate in the rain and scatter in the wind. He came by every day, but eventually he stopped coming.

I see him far less regularly now. When I glimpsed him last, he was carving his way through the park pushing a shopping trolley full of green bags with straight and determined arms.

A Real Piece of Work

'I'm going to kill someone here in a minute, I'm fucking raging, but!' Bobby says to me.

Bobby's a Scotsman and has been here forty years though his accent remains strong – his is a voice that is at once gruff and golden.

I am sitting in a floral-patterned water-resistant bucket chair. The kind of chair familiar to anyone who's ever been inside a nursing home. If someone pisses on this kind of chair, it sits, mercury-like, atop the fabric until someone sees it and slides it right off.

We don't call it a nursing home, though.

We gloss over this brutal phrasing with more ambiguous language, in the work that I do. Residential aged care facility. Hostel. Low level aged care. 'Place a bit like a hospital but more like a home,' was the description I often gave to my clients. If 'like a home' is living with seventy strangers in a huge compound and sharing a room with people you've never met.

Bobby's a seasoned roller of darts; his fingers are yellowed at the tips. His fingernails are long and dirty – matched only by toenails that curl right around the edges of his toes. He's cranky because he's been told he can only smoke 50 metres down the street – opposite the bus stop. He struggles with the walk. (Those toes.)

Bobby moved into the nursing home a few weeks earlier. I'd helped him find the place, even though he's too good, too functional, too worldly, for a place like this. Without it, however, he wouldn't survive Sydney rent. He'd be homeless. Bobby is also here, in this nursing home, because his partner Shirl is here.

Bobby was referred to me by a community support worker who described Bobby as a 'real piece of work'. 'He's been to jail, you know?' they said, without a hint of irony. As if we spoke the same language.

Shirl had dementia and her previous case manager, via the usual institutional state channels, had advocated for a guardian and trustee to be appointed to make decisions on her behalf. For years before that Bobby and Shirl had thrown their pensions together and survived this way. Just.

When Shirl arrived at the nursing home she wasn't wearing any undies, just, strangely, a gravity-defying continence pad. As she stood it fell to the ground with a wet thud. Bobby lovingly bent down and picked up the pad as if it were an umbrella left on a bus.

Every payday he'd trek to Frangos in Petersham and return with Portuguese charcoal chicken and seemingly endless hot chips. I knew how much he adored Shirl when I found that out – the line for Frangos was always out the door, the place a Sydney institution. I'd sit, swallowed by the floral-patterned water-resistant bucket chair, and watch Shirl hungrily devour Bobby's greasy offerings of love.

Before the nursing home, Shirl had been in hospital for almost half a year and before that, in social housing in Western Sydney. Bobby was struggling to look after her. Sometimes she was so confused that she found him unrecognisable and wouldn't let him into her unit after he'd taken the train an hour to see her. She would slam the door in his face and threaten to call the police.

This is a hard story to tell because so much of my work with older people in the community is private, confidential. I cannot share whole stories, because they do not belong to me. And so, this story is an amalgam of many, the context changed, people unrecognisable, de-identified, made invisible again.

Social work is about centring the person, their desires and dreams for their own lives. It means being trusted with treasured stories of resilience and strength, to tread lightly with the stories of others. Whose story gets to be told and who gets to tell it?

I also have a role to play in ensuring systems are challenged. If we cannot tell the stories of people failed, of the interplay of factors that have influenced and limited people's dreams, we are failing at one of the most fundamental roles social workers have, which is to uphold justice.

It is in stories that we can centre lives affected by systemic injustice. That we unearth problems that need fixing. I think we can find ways to tell these kinds of stories.

For seven years I have been working this job where I burrow, momentarily, into the middle of people's lives. The work has gifted me opportunities to hear the stories of people I'd not know in another life. To be let in like this has been both one of the most magical experiences of my life and the most distressing. Being let in means witnessing that wealth and power do not trickle down to those most vulnerable. It is to see oppressed people made more marginal in a system that only benefits the few. Being let in comes with the brutal realisation that change as you want to see it – as these people most need change – will not happen in this lifetime.

Working in the community, where there are so few supports for the very old and isolated, makes it hard to reconcile the social work values I hold close – those of social justice, human dignity, opportunity of access, a life safe from violence – with the brutal reality that they are so difficult to achieve, to mete out, in a capitalist system so fundamentally unjust.

Bobby receives the aged pension, $1026.50 per fortnight. The poverty line, for an adult in Australia, is $978 per fortnight. To live in an aged care facility in Australia, for someone like Bobby, costs 85 per cent of this pension. After fees are paid, which cover food, rent and healthcare (but not medications), the person is left with $153.97 every fortnight.

The week after Bobby and Shirl's move, I scoured the two-dollar shop for the largest and most comfortable-looking ladies' underpants I could find. Cottontail rip-offs. I found them in purple, beige and pink. I found some singlets, too. Singlets like sails.

I punched in the code, wrote my name in the visitors' book and took the lift that lurched uneasily to the sixth floor of the labyrinthine nursing home. A muffled classical fuzz drifted from the ancient relic stereo that Bobby had rescued from someone's hard rubbish. Shirl and Bobby were screaming over it like two people trying to have a serious conversation at the club. Shirl's muumuu revealed half of her enormous breasts. Hands full of morning tea. Eyes bright. 'Pleasure to see you!' she chirped.

I placed the undies and the singlets neatly on the arm of the water-resistant bucket chair. I encouraged Shirl to try them on as a way to keep her pads in.

The idea that a vulnerable older woman can go to a nursing home from hospital, with barely any follow-up from a case-worker, without underpants and with no accessible money, is one I find hard to sit with. But it happens all the time. Sure, Shirl needed a financial manager: managing her money was a complex task that she really could not do anymore, but as a process, the paperwork takes weeks, sometimes months. There is rarely an interim plan.

This is not an uncommon story. Due to the substantial cuts to case management and community supports for older people in Australia – which were essentially all but wiped out by the 2015 Aged Care Reforms – most of the older people I work with, especially those who are impaired, vulnerable or without families, are institutionalised early if they can no longer safely live alone. It's not uncommon to hear of someone going from hospital into care without ever returning home to collect their things.

When I first met Shirl, she was sitting bolt upright in her hospital bed. She'd made friends with the three other older women in her four-bedded room. They were all quite confused, and Shirl, least confused of the four, was often re-directing the others back to their own beds. Her own community case manager had disappeared and so, given I was linked with Bobby, I took her on, too.

This happens a lot in the sector. Clinicians, mostly well-intentioned, underpaid, overworked and time-limited, hope that someone else will catch their clients when they land in hospital. Resources have been cut and services 'streamlined', and the way you might have done something, the time you might have had – you don't even have half of it anymore.

I met Bobby for the first time at the dingy hospital cafeteria. He had a phone but seemed unable to work out how to answer it, and any time I called I was met with static and background noise. I soon learnt that he visited Shirl most days. The physiotherapists had worked out that only Bobby could encourage Shirl to get out of bed and do her rehab exercises that might get her mobile enough to be discharged from hospital. And so, that's where I went to get to know him.

He'd always show up.

Bobby. Bobby the piece of work. Bobby with his collection of knives and his history.

'You know what he did, don't you?'

'He's resourceful, he'll manage.'

'He's a personality disorder, for sure. He can sort himself out.'

'They shouldn't be housed in the same nursing home if that's ultimately where they wind up,' someone else, I forget now, pitched to me.

Bobby and Shirl had been together for fifteen years. At the mention of them being separated, Bobby turned to me and said, 'It's like they're stealing her all over again.'

And here I am. Placing Shirl into a nursing home.

Here I am. A white settler social worker who believes themself radical, who understands that structural violence and institutionalised racism and poverty and colonisation and intergenerational trauma are all at play in this moment, here I am placing a First Nations woman into another institution.

This is the only option available at this moment, because of Shirl's high level nursing care needs. In the aged care system we have, if you have money, you can instantly access care. For those with very little, like Bobby and Shirl, they are reliant on government-subsidised care. Vulnerable poor people end up in care early, mainly because the community services they need are months away from being accessible. There isn't enough of it.

I think about older bodies, how they are seen as devalued and unprofitable bodies under capitalism. I think about the system as it is and its lack of alternatives for those with so little. How in a moment like this, the limit to what you can do is so striking because the crisis, born of years of injustice, is already there in front of you.

This is not to let myself off the hook, to say not much can be done in the moment. The unpicking of injustice and structural oppression is so multi-layered. But I know that I cannot in my work with Shirl, undo it all. I can't *not* place her in the institution, because if I don't, she would be homeless.

I have long sat with the despondency of being unable to fix structural problems in the face-to-face rapport-building work that is the greatest skill I possess. More recently, I found solace in the work of Canadian social justice activist and psychotherapist Vikki Reynolds. Reynolds speaks about 'unhappenings' – the immeasurable outcomes of community work with the most marginal, the things that do not happen because workers are involved: supporting people where they are at, the crises averted, the suicides prevented, the nursing homes found and the cyclical hospitalisations thwarted.[1] In a time of productivity, of measuring 'success', of key performance indicators – it is little wonder community workers often experience feelings of burnout, when their work, in this context, is rendered invisible. It's only now, as community work has been substantially de-funded, that we can actually see how much this 'invisible' work matters and how big its loss actually is to those living on society's edges.

Reynolds's concept of 'unhappenings' was a helpful re-frame for me at a time I most needed it. It is a way to both value the work and stay present and hopeful within it. It reminds me of the important responsibility we have on the individual level to our clients. The responsibility to connect the micro to the macro.

We must hold in mind, always, the forces that shape disadvantage and perpetuate injustice. To see our clients – who have bravely carved out lives in the shadows of structures that would crush them – as strong, wise and resilient people from whom we have much to learn. Under capitalism, not everyone can participate in the market. They cannot simply try harder.

Individualising people's problems conceals the role that state-based violence plays and perpetuates daily. Reynolds tells us that it is not the clients who burn us out, but the systems that they exist within that create the challenges they continue to face. Structures that affect and challenge us in our work as clinicians and in our lives outside of work. To know this is to ensure we try, in every word, action and intervention, not to re-enact this power imbalance anymore – when we are in the room and with our clients.

The last time I visited the nursing home, the cottontail rip-offs and the singlets had vanished from the arm of the bucket chair. I looked to Shirl, asked her how they fit.

'I'm fookin' loving them!' Bobby piped up, shooting me a face full of yellowing, joyful teeth as he shifted his shirt and trackie bottoms a bit, revealing some high-waisted pink undies and a fresh new singlet. And, despite my best intentions to dilute the power dynamic between us, it remained fixed. Our stories for life had long been structurally predestined, Bobby, Shirl and I, sealing us into such strikingly divergent paths. I got to leave the nursing home that day, in my work car, all too aware of the distance left to travel between a system that's just and the one we're in.

COVID Exercise Bike

Between March 2020, when COVID-19 enveloped communities in fear, and August 2020, as a second wave of infections had us retreating once more, I purchased three exercise bikes.

When the world was different I had a rigid, routine life that involved the gym, the pool and the occasional pump class before work. My exercising had its own daily rhythm. I would take selfies in the bathroom mirror, put them on Instagram and inhale the dopamine hit that came from the flurry of likes, love heart eyes and fire emojis. Virtual poppers going straight to my head. The validation of the genderqueer body.

My gym-going, while not really a secret, was one I guarded. I never spoke about how long or how often I was there. How significantly organised my life was around exercise. I didn't talk about how it functioned as a cheap way to regulate my feelings of dysphoria. Dysphoria around my body, my gender and how they coexisted.

I didn't speak to the thoughts I had that if I didn't go, my body would transmogrify into something grotesque. I held close to my tiny chest shameful feelings that intellectually and socially, I knew were unspeakable. The feelings that gave energy to the values I did not wish to hold – fatphobic, ableist ones that ran counter to the body-positive, woke queer I believed myself to be. While I didn't believe anyone else needed to fit narrowly defined, socially prescribed standards of beauty and attractiveness, I held an unreachable bar for myself.

My gym-going, lap-swimming and pump class-attending gave rhythm to my life and buttressed the container that held so much in. Exercising made my body liveable.

I used to live opposite a swimming pool and a gym. Before lockdown, my social media feed teemed with information about how if Australia was going to flatten the curve, we needed to be socially distancing. Staying away from places where people gathered. Places like gyms and pools. Like many anxious people, I was infuriated by others' seemingly wilful ignorance, their blatant disregard for the safety and health of others. Weeks before lockdown, I wrote exasperated posts on Facebook, encouraging friends to think critically, to change their behaviour. I spent an entire afternoon constructing an enormous cardboard sign and stuck it to the bedroom window in a desperate attempt to inspire people to stay at home. I saw passers-by squinting up to read it. A man took a photo of it with his phone.

While all this was happening, I was deeply troubled by the collapse of my routine. I cancelled my gym membership and retreated into my apartment. I was angry with but jealous of these people disappearing in and out of the gym, attending to their routines. I needed mine, too, but something much bigger was at stake. My dysphoria-maintenance routine had been short-circuited by a global pandemic.

It is interesting to think about it now, that it was the needs of others, and not my own mental health, that inspired my premature retreat. A theme that has simmered throughout my life is that the needs and comfort of other people come first. My routine, unchanged and unchallenged in many years, was over in a day.

So I bought exercise bike number one.

When bike number one came, I realised it was a small toy disguised as a piece of fitness equipment. I had been fooled by an internet sale and, realising no rigorous exercise would be happening on its fragile frame, I dipped into my dwindling savings and purchased a name-brand spin bike. I hoped that by splurging I'd avoid similar disappointment.

As a younger person, I held onto a warped notion of what my body looked like. I say warped because I had so little choice and few models for what was possible for a body to be. As someone coming of age pre-internet, the idea that I had just two genders to choose from, in order to try and 'succeed' in the body I had been born and socialised into – didn't help me much with my body problems. I had a hard time meeting the standards of the gender the world had so effortlessly placed on me and I wore it for decades like an ill-fitting shirt.

These narratives around crafting and maintaining the 'perfect' body permeate queer culture in such invasive ways, even though so many of us often don't fulfil the normative ideas circulating around us of gender or bodies. Our bodies, to many, so far from perfect – out of line, illegible, other.

I remember my mother's bitter disappointment so vividly when one night I arrived at my parents' house with a fresh fade. Her face visibly pained, her tone acrid and crushing: 'Why do you have to make yourself so unattractive?' To her, nothing was more unattractive than a feminine masculinity.

My distress around how much I was exercising or the thoughts that I was failing to deconstruct the powers I believed I was immune to didn't leave much room for a more compassionate reading. There wasn't space to interrogate what else I had been trying to achieve, control and manage. Anti-fatness and ableism defy gender lines and are deeply rooted in a society and culture that celebrates and socially rewards non-queer, non-trans, non-feminine bodies. I, like many people, wasn't immune to dangerous cultural messaging – from which certain themes stand out. Certain bodies hold currency.

Exercise bike number two arrived. Sturdy and sleek. I put on my grey bike shorts, took my spin class internet subscription into the garage and lowered the electronic garage door. I pedalled a lot at 'racing resistance' and 'standing attack' in the dark to my new favourite spin class instructors Glen, Dee and Brent from Les Mills On Demand. I started to hear the pulsating cover tracks in my head. My pandemic plan B was underway.

Much of my exercising has been less about meeting certain standards placed upon bodies (though I think I have been held hostage by these dangerous myths for years), and more about trying to transform it. It is a new realisation; one deeply rooted in long having felt uneasy in my skin. Of course, there is the enjoyable aspect of being fit and well, healthy and mobile, but for me, the shadow side of this was obsessive and clinical. As if in going to the gym enough, being hard enough in my body, being buff, getting more buff, some of the feelings of dysphoria, the ones I did not wish to entertain, could be curtailed.

The gym and exercise *was* my gender affirmation. I intellectualised it as a version of the medically assisted transition I was yearning for but not willing to admit to wanting for myself. So, the daily ritual, much like taking hormones, was an aspect of affirming my gender every day. One I was hopeful was 'enough'. So much about the policing of my queer body via regimented exercise was about transforming my gender. A way of convincing myself that I was doing something about it.

I had somehow conned myself into the belief that the gym would allow me to transition in the ways I wanted to, inside the gender assigned to me by others – as if by magic. As if in working out hard enough, I would be read by the world around me as the person I knew myself to be, who was not a woman and not a man, plus I could do this without distressing anyone – mostly my parents, who I knew might be most distressed of all. And so, for years I was bench-pressing into an idea of myself.

And then, mid-mountain climb, the resistance knob of the second exercise bike stopped working. I was devastated.

Three weeks and forty-six email exchanges between the internet gym-equipment provider and myself later, exercise bike number three arrived.

I unpacked the new bike the day it arrived, one wintry afternoon.

My neighbour Akira is ten years old and lives with her mum in the unit below. I see her in the stairwell some mornings when she is going to school. The last time I saw her I was on the second spin bike pedalling furiously and she caught me with the garage door open. I quickly stopped. 'You're so fast and strong!' she said, which I found cute and encouraging. I got off and walked over to her. She had her bag packed and was going to a friend's house for her first ever sleepover.

I recognised in Akira something I remember in myself as a small person – a desire to be noticed by adults. To please, to be seen, to be found interesting. She often wanders into the garage when she sees me in there. We talk about school, television shows, food we love. How I find it impressive that she can speak two languages while I have only one. She asked one of those innocent questions only children can about age – asking who was the eldest of my housemate and I. Before I could answer, she candidly told me she thought I was 'the young one'. I told her frankly that I was probably the same age as her mum and she point-blank would not have it.

As I was assembling exercise bike number three, Akira skipped into the garage. We pieced the bike together. I handed her the Allen key, we consulted the manual, she screwed bits into place and I moved out of her way so she could lie down and screw the pedals on.

As we were tinkering with the bike, I remembered the small version of myself. How meaningful it was when I was noticed, talked to as if I was special. I remember how my heart swelled. When we'd finished, Akira and I got up and dusted off our knees.

'Are you a boy or a girl?' Akira asked out of the blue as I was peeling lint from my tracksuit pants.

'I'm a bit of both,' came my reply.

'I thought that!' Akira said enthusiastically.

I appreciated that her curiosity about my gender was something that came to her an hour into our bike-tinkering. That it wasn't so important. Out in the world where binary understandings of gender are still so pronounced, there seems to be a need for other people, mostly cisgender people, to decipher and categorise gender-diverse people in order to understand. As if until they can clock us through the limited lenses conventional culture affords them, the words coming out of our mouths are gibberish – made comprehensible only through the other person's skilful ability to box us into something knowable.

The replacement bike was repositioned in the back of the garage and Akira mounted her own small orange BMX. She put on her helmet. I'd seen her trying to learn to ride her new bike in the common area outside the unit block before, though I didn't let her know. I didn't tell her I had seen her straddling the seat with her tip-toes on the ground, periodically shrieking when she thought she was about to fall off.

'Watch me!' she ordered. I was ten years old when I learnt to ride a bike, I told her. I watched her and I said some encouraging words as I stood there in my tracksuit pants and smiled as she played. She turned back to make sure I was still watching. I was the adult and she the small me, desperate to be seen. It is an easy gift and I valued my newfound job, to remind her that she is special, important and clever.

I didn't tell Akira about the time I was ten and had finally mastered my Malvern Star with the flowery banana seat, when my mum took me to the bike park and I rode around in my red monochrome tracksuit and a group of boys shouted at me, sarcastically, 'Nice bike!'. I didn't tell her that I rode back to Mum, full of shame, put the bike down at her feet and asked to go home. How I never once rode it again.

After a few brave pedal-strokes, Akira found her pace and at the last minute saved herself from toppling.

For a long time, internalised transphobia gripped me tightly, as did my desperate need to demonstrate that women can look like me – they can straddle the in-between and walk the edges of gender. My desire to be a model for others outstripped my need to be honest with myself about how I actually felt about being a woman in the world. Even a butch one. It never felt like me, but the idea of medically assisted transition to being read as a man in the world wasn't me either, though I thought about it often.

I told myself that it was a gift to be a woman in the world. That I had a big job to carry out. I told myself that I was comfortable being a woman and even if I wasn't, it was an important body to be born into. There was much work to do in deconstructing ideas of what women can be, I reminded myself. Despite the fact I felt uneasy in my body for years, I repeated this story so often I believed it to be true.

Thinking about transitioning medically, to find my place in the middle, for a long time felt like I would be reneging on something I'd promised the world, in all those years of self-denial. I worried it would solidify homophobic and transphobic ideas in other people that all butch women just want to be men. That it was misogynist of me if I couldn't deconstruct that patriarchy had conditioned me into needing and wanting the masculinity that was just a construction anyway. I told myself that focusing on the individual who was already privileged enough was unimportant – there were greater injustices that needed my attention. Transition, pronouns, making space for new, re-fashioned and (re) affirming versions of oneself was always something for other people – but never something for me.

On reflection, my exercising was confining the possibility of what my life could look like. I saw myself change with exercise but not in the ways I wanted most. I didn't want to be seen as a man, but I was so consistently distressed whenever I was referred to as a woman, as a 'lady'. It disturbed, so profoundly, the image I held of myself. So, while in my rational brain, I knew the gym would never afford me the moustache I wanted, the deeper voice, the hardened frame – features I could not manifest on the elliptical machine – I convinced myself that it was enough.

Like everyone, I understand myself through a mediated world. One in which social and cultural shifts impact how we understand ourselves in relation to others. We are influenced and shaped by the representations around us. For most of my life, the physical and material reality of it provided so few options in which to see myself reflected. I didn't see any genderqueer kids on television, in books or magazines.

I didn't see many gay characters on the television either, and when I did, they were mostly all I had. While gender may be a construction, how it has been crafted in the world influences how we understand ourselves in very real ways. So, while I have been a non-binary person my entire life, this understanding was far outside of my grasp, in both language and real-world possibility. It wasn't an option because I did not see it. I have never been a girl or a boy, a woman or a man – though for years tried to squeeze myself into one of them because it was the closest fit.

The last three years has been a time of great shifts. I have begun to see myself as worthy. It has taken many years of therapy but I have learnt to say no. No to things I don't wish to do, no to things that take away from what is important to me. No to things done out of obligation, to please others. I have learnt to love myself.

Doing things for other people, in my work as a social worker and in my personal life, was a constant theme. The idea of sticking to being a woman in the world was for other people. Not indulging the possibilities of affirming my gender, moving towards something authentic. That, too, was for other people.

On Christmas Day 2019 I took testosterone for the first time. I began a new daily ritual: gifting myself the small grace of affirming who I already am. In some respects, it was a move long overdue, a simmering desire held in place by an unchallenged ritual disrupted by a pandemic.

The unfolding comedy of the malfunctioning bikes and the entry of a small ten-year-old bike-tinkering messenger was the gift I didn't know I needed. A reminder of the deeper things that need more attention and care than just being contained. The time afforded by the pandemic gave me the space to think more about the function of exercise in my life. Underneath it, a deep knowledge was waiting for its time.

Liv Tyler

In 2018 I went on a holiday to Vancouver. I went to visit my American ex and my friends from the Pacific Northwest who were willing to cross the border to see me. The previous year, I'd moved to Olympia, Washington, to see if living in the same place as my partner could be the life for me. Three weeks in, I was refused entry back into the US after a weekend in Canada because I had some anarchist books in my bag.

'Have you smoked marijuana?'

'Have you been looking for work?'

'What is this antifa book?'

Border control agents left me alone in a room for hours, put a stamp in my passport forbidding my return.

I was grateful I hadn't yet made a life in America. I cried uncontrollably on the Canadian side of the border knowing my relationship was over. A sweet queer anarchist from Montreal who had gone for a gay weekend in Seattle bent down and handed me four cigarettes which I chain-smoked out of the sunroof of my friend's van as we drove back to her house overlooking the sea.

My experience was not so bad, really. I was white and I hadn't lived in the US for years, unlike so many people who had made full livelihoods in America only to be deported at the whim of racist border policing. That's the story of how my American ex became my American ex who is now my American friend, whom I think about sometimes, but not very often. It's not this story, though.

This story is the story of how I was a slut in 2017 and how it led me to Vancouver in early 2018 to see my favourite Americans and then to Montreal to have sex with a beautiful woman who was Liv Tyler's doppelganger. It was the other side of the country to my planned Vancouver holiday but it was the same continent, so I decided to see Liv Tyler, too.

I had already had sex a few times with Liv Tyler, who was originally from Australia but was making a living as an artist in the US. The first time was at my house when she had come to Australia for Christmas. The next morning, I drove her to a coffee shop to meet friends before she flew back to LA. I kissed her by the side of my new car and wished her a Merry Christmas. The second and third and fourth time was in February when she'd returned to Australia for a friend's wedding.

I didn't anticipate seeing Liv Tyler again. She added me on Instagram and we sent nudes to each other and spoke on the phone sometimes. She sent me some emails and I wrote long-winded, attentive replies. I projected a few things onto Liv Tyler. She had recently cut off most of her hair. It was once much longer, like when she was in the film *Empire Records*.

If I was going to Canada anyway, Liv Tyler suggested we meet somewhere on the North American continent. I liked having sex with Liv Tyler and I wanted to do it again – even if just for a week. So, after my week with the Americans in a cabin on an island in Vancouver, I found Liv Tyler in Montreal.

From the taxi, I watched Liv Tyler climb down the icy steps of an apartment block, trailing a giant leopard print patterned wheelie bag that bounced rhythmically behind her. It had been weeks since I had seen Liv Tyler. Her skin was smooth and clear and her short dark hair was slick and sharp. Large golden hooped earrings offset her black monochrome. She smiled and hers was a face filled with desire, excitement and hope.

I wanted to continue my soft re-entry into the world of queer dating, which had been such a refreshing time for me after my US banishment. I had come back to Australia and in that year of mending my broken heart I had spent a lot of time reading and being by myself. I had also made a Tinder profile, gone to a bunch of parties and on occasion, went home with hot strangers.

I went on some cute dates. I spent time with a woman who slept on a mattress on the floor, illuminated by a salt lamp. She liked to read poetry, called me a faggot and treated me like one, and left me sleeping while she trained for a half marathon before sunrise. I dated a doctor and we saw each other infrequently for sex and a cuddle and I learnt about how people navigate open relationships and can be so decent to one another, even when they are anxious and afraid of change but want to try something new. I had a booty call with a woman

I met in a line for tickets to a party. I went over to her house, crawled out at 3 am and never saw her again. A friend asked if we could have a sex date, and I was astonished by her incredibly brazen offer and we made a time for 11 am on a Thursday at my house. I made a cup of tea for us beforehand.

At thirty-two I discovered party drugs and the ways in which I could communicate effectively with people and make space for the healing I'd never done. I was experiencing a peak period of sexual liberation about ten years too late but I was enjoying having it. I felt so far removed from the people-pleasing version of myself who often made decisions with the motivating factor being not to hurt anyone. In doing life this way I had mostly hurt myself.

I took this version of myself to Montreal. I was ready for a cute time in this wintery, francophone city with its easy to navigate crisscross of streets and to visit Drawn and Quarterly, the comic bookshop of my dreams. I was excited to see Liv Tyler. She knew about my lovers back home and the openness in which I had found such liberation. Her mouth said she was fine; her eyes, though, communicated a glassy sadness.

The Airbnb was cosy. The balcony was slicked with a fine coat of snow. This was what couples did together, I realised. They rented Airbnbs in cute cities and had cute holidays and had sex some days before venturing out. I was hoping that we could do nice things together, as people into each other, queers with no plans beyond this. I imagined we would climb Mount Royal happily together in the snow and take a photo at the top.

We worked out very early in our week in Montreal that we wanted different things. My disinterest in something big was painful to Liv Tyler and our intimacy felt heavy. Most days we split up. I rambled the city looking for bagels and bookshops and wrote postcards to my friends. I found my lover with the mattress on the floor's old house and sent her a photo of me on the doorstep smiling and pointing to the number on the apartment door. Liv Tyler worked on her computer in the cafe. I found a local gym and it was a workout in itself getting in and out of so many layers of clothes. Liv Tyler and I ate vegan poutine in silence.

'I don't want to go to Toronto anymore,' Liv Tyler announced from where she sat, cross-legged on the edge of the bed, her laptop light illuminating her face in the darkened room. She rebooked her flight back to New York for the following morning. I was relieved and would finish my time in Montreal alone. The last time I saw Liv Tyler, she was crying on the corner of Fairmont and Jeanne-Mance as she disappeared in a taxi headed for the airport.

Two hours after the taxi left the kerb, a francophone DJ and speed-dating hostess chose me out of a sea of faces on her phone.

I find her at the print shop, 5678 ave du Parc, stoned and wearing enormous clomp-y shoes. She is printing posters for her next lesbian dating event. I hand over black coffee in a paper cup and we walk to Chinatown together where we eat.

She is the daughter of a Haitian man and her mother became her mother after having sex just once on a beach. Heather the francophone DJ. We walk to the queer bar where she hosts her weekly singles night which is not on this night but is on Thursdays.

Heather tells me all about her penchant for freaks. I'm a freak though she doesn't know that because she used all the air to talk. We eat slices of pizza and Heather knows most people at the bar. She is like a real lesbian celebrity, sashaying around the room, introducing me to Canadian queers I'll never see again. I ask if I can kiss her but she says that she's too anxious.

We farewell at 2 am on an icy corner and I return to the Airbnb of broken dreams.

Heather the francophone DJ texts me. I'm eating corn-flakes on the couch.

If you feel like coming over,
you can

I'm from Australia, I'll get lost.

I want to touch your hair.

And so, on my last night in Montreal, Heather the franco-phone DJ comes over and strokes my hair until we fall asleep. On the screen where it all began, she says that it was a blessing to have spent the night with a hot prince in an Ikea palace.

Heather the francophone DJ and I are still friends on the internet. Liv Tyler wrote me an email with nothing in the body. The subject line read: stop following me on Instagram please thank you. With no punctuation.

The Darlinghurst Discount

We weren't in Darlinghurst when we got the Darlinghurst Discount. We were deep in Sydney's factory-outlet promised land: Alexandria.

If someone had told me that one day, I would be buying a bed at a homemaker centre, looking into my future's bright blue eyes, as the electronic mattress profiler whirred into gear, lowered by a charismatic queer man called Larry – I'd have said fuck right off.

In the past, I had never been able to see what was ahead, to make plans for the future. My relationships, the romantic ones at least, often felt so precarious. Buying a bed with someone indicated a real investment in each other. A willingness to stick around.

You, at thirty-seven, had never bought a new bed. Always collected from the side of the road or forwarded on by upwardly mobile friends. Too much of an investment for someone who had moved around so much and never planned to settle down. Who, like me, believed that every relationship would end and went into new relationships with the hope of enjoying things while they lasted. Forever until it wasn't any fun anymore.

But you had landed, back in Sydney and after floating on the periphery of one another's lives for more than a decade we found in each other a certainty never known before

We were buying our new bed with money from our parents. Yours had bought your three brothers' beds as wedding gifts. This extravagance was something you never believed would be extended to you. Yet so much had shifted in the time between then and my meeting you.

It is an odd gift. The buying of a bed for your adult child. The adult child who will, presumably, go on for many years fucking and sleeping on it.

And so, we found ourselves at the homemaker centre one gloomy weekend mid-afternoon. Both anxious people, we liked the idea of trialling beds and working it out on our own. But then we met Larry. Larry with his bulbous belly, his familiar charm and his deeply comforting queerness.

'Are you side or tummy sleepers?' Larry quizzed us.

'I'm often referred to as a beautiful log,' I reply, craning my neck in your direction, referencing your apt description of my default tummy sleep position.

'I can imagine,' he flirted back.

We told him you liked to mix it up – a versatile sleeper.

Larry sometimes spoke of himself in the third person which was oddly comforting. He looked a bit like a gay Alec Baldwin.

'Don't worry, Larry's going to look after you. I'm going to give you the Darlinghurst Discount!'

There is something deeply pleasurable in being seen and read as queer by those of the same ilk. The subtle references, the furtive nods on the street, an acknowledgement of shared otherness. Larry didn't need to say any more than that, his Darlinghurst Discount screamed 'I see you, I'm an absolute freak too! We must look after each other!' We lapped up our momentary gay privilege.

We engaged in theatrical recreations of our own night-life on the many mattresses. I flung myself onto the bed, face down, perched stiff as a board, you with your butt softly resting against my leg. In between our bedroom calisthenics, Larry perched on the edge of a nearby bed and we talked about sleep. I had just finished a book on the science of sleep and was now determined to give myself an eight-hour sleep window after discovering that sleep debt can never be repaid. Larry got ten hours a night. He told us the benefits of the $200 mattress protector that he would be giving us for free. 'It's great if you enjoy drinking wine in bed,' he said. I wondered about Larry's sleep hygiene and considered lending him my book.

We spoke about the pros and cons of ensemble base versus bed frame. Larry preferred ensembles. He didn't even have a 'skirt' for his. He had simply repurposed a black double fitted sheet.

'How important is easy access to three sides of the bed for you?' Larry asked.

'Vital!' came our enthusiastic reply.

God he was good. I looked at you and your bright blue eyes smiled back at me.

I had long held shame about being queer and kept partners at arm's length from my family. Years of therapy had dislodged the shame and the more I liked myself, the more my outsider status was intolerable. I found compassion for my parents and understood the ways in which socialised norms had infected them with dangerous myths. Myths that families either replicate or reject. Queers who fitted into mainstream cultural imaginings of gender and sexuality were tolerable for them, but me, with my rough edges, left them in a sort of existential parental distress. Therefore our parents' collective bed-buying, symbolically, meant a lot. Their investment, quite literally, in our gay sex, the ultimate act of contrition.

Having redeemed our Darlinghurst Discount, we left the homemaker centre with a renewed faith in family. Larry was a simple reminder that capitalism fucks us all, especially those living more marginal lives like queers – who are often more precariously employed, less privileged. Larry didn't know us, but his willingness to carve into inflated prices for two queer freaks was a benevolent reminder that queer family runs deep, with ready access to all sides of the bed.

The Moments in Which I Love You are too Numerous, but Here are Some of Them

That time, not long after we met, when I complained that my baby pink sweatshirt had stains on it, despite furious washing, that just wouldn't come out. I came home from work and you told me to close my eyes and into my outstretched palms you placed the baby pink sweatshirt minus all its grotty stains. Perfectly folded. It was one of the most beautiful things anyone had ever done for me.

When you suggested we fuck when I got home from the shops. I hadn't been in and out of a supermarket so fast. I came through the door of our flat to you wrapped in a towel. I placed the groceries on the kitchen bench and turned to you. You tilted your head in the direction of our room. 'Hurry up,' it said.

The leftover olives. Two perfectly round, crisp green ones, some salty kalamatas floating in a tiny bowl. I ate a few of the kalamatas and left one green one for you. I tell you that there are some olives left for you. I come back to a half-eaten green olive. 'That half's yours,' you say. Not knowing we had the same idea.

I was nervous on our second date. I had not seen you in three whole weeks. Three weeks that were the longest, most exciting and excruciating of my life. I walked the steps to your apartment and I stood at the front door for a moment before knocking. You opened the door in the most magnificent black outfit. We did not greet each other with words, but walked towards each other and kissed one another so tenderly for so long. It was the moment I knew that I loved you. It was the defining kiss of my lifetime. If there is a memory I will have when I am close to my end – this will be it.

Your hands. Hands so elegant and soft. I watch your hands in the world and I am mesmerised. There is so much kindness in those hands.

The December when, every morning for twelve days in the lead-up to Christmas, you would send me one of twelve perfect nudes. The advent calendar of my dreams. The photographs you'd taken on your phone at the Airbnb in between my making breakfast and going to the shop for painkillers.

The way, when talking to other people about me, you speak of me as they, as if it is the most effortless fit. In watching you hold space for me, stretching other people's minds while also opening yourself up for critique, love overtakes me because in this moment, I notice how much I matter.

Curled up on our bed, watching a show and you mime a door-knock and I know to lift my arm so that we can be closer.

At some point the robot vacuum cleaner has become 'our child' and continues to swallow computer cables and phone chargers. I smile at you because you'll say things like 'Our child got into the spare room' or 'I'll get our child to clean the floor after dinner'. Sometimes we hate our child and put it upside down on the couch.

The drive home from Lithgow. Singing 'Dreams' by Gabrielle and imagining all the songs we will play at the wedding. Also on our minds is the karaoke party. What will we sing? '"Tubthumping" by Chumbwumba,' I suggest. We sing – no, chant – it loudly, between smiles as wide as our love, all the way home. I park the car on the corner of our block. We unpack the car and you kiss me, tenderly, my hands at my sides, full of bags.

The way, on finishing a book, you rise to collect your diary, rifle to its final page and add another title to the books you've read this year.

I felt faint walking up the stairs to the front door. Bags in my hands. You open the door to my face without colour and lay me down on the golden couch. With your beautiful, kind nurse hands, you count my pulse. Forty beats per minute.

A vasovagal, you think. You call your dad. The doctor agrees. You prop my feet upon a pillow and deliver me toast with peanut butter. You sit next to me and we laugh because I'd taken too much beta blocker.

Our game 'open or closed', where you guess whether my very small eyes are open or closed. It is most fun when, early in the morning, the difference is a slither no thicker than an eyelash and you, devilishly, refer to my clearly open eyes as 'CLOSED'.

Words and how they form in your mouth. Put together in combinations soft and measured. Your poetry of the everyday. You look at me, in wonder. After knowing so much of my story, you remind me how incredible it is that I have grown myself into the person that I am.

I live between my apartment and our apartment. It was once your apartment but now we share it and it is the place we call 'home'. I took the oversized monstera down from the top shelf at work and it now lives in our bedroom where every few weeks you gently point out its unfurling baby leaves. We cook in our small corner kitchen and read on the golden couch in silence and sometimes we raise our heads and let our eyes speak words we don't have. On Saturdays I take our coffee cups down the street to the cafe where the barista knows the coffees for each cup. I bring them back and place them on the side table and I put my inside pants back on and I climb back into the warmth of your arms.

*

The red-brick corner block next to the pool. The pool where, for years, late at night I took myself to recharge after days spent supporting other people. A lane to myself, I would glide up and down, with only numbers in my head. Swimming, not drowning, made beautiful. Leaving the pool, I would look to the red-brick corner block with its lights and windows for eyes. A dull pink illuminating the room of someone I didn't know. And then I fell in love with you. You, who lives in the red-brick corner block with its windows like eyes.

The beach was windy the first time I fully experienced your pathological aversion to sand. You sat in the back of the car and I painstakingly wiped your feet clean with your special sand-proof towel – as if it was the greatest task anyone had ever entrusted me with. I imagined my new life as a podiatrist and you took a video of me at your feet and said it was the most loving thing I'd ever done for you. We laughed so much driving home that I had a hard time seeing the road.

You send me a text asking if I'm alone. You wanted to send me a video you'd made. I put down my pen, got up and closed the blinds. I opened the text message and pressed play on the video. It was your toenail on the brink of collapse. I was at once disappointed – my hands had drifted south in anticipation, though I'd fast removed them in a fit of laughter. A lifelong picker of toes: 'I'd like to have a go at that tonight' I texted back. You said it was getting hard to hang on but that you would try and hold out for me.

*

Visiting Doug and Dulcie, your beautiful grandparents, in their mid-nineties and still so independent, on the hottest, driest Melbourne weekend in January. We jumped into Aunt Helen's four-wheel drive and went to the lawyers and Kmart and to test out recliner chairs at the independent equipment specialist. We sat in the mini seats up the back, teenagers again. We held hands and you mouthed 'I love you'.

In the evenings, in their matching brown recliners, Dulcie would very loudly read the news's closed captions to deaf Doug with added emphasis on the serious stories and dire weather warnings. In the mornings Dulcie would rise and prepare breakfast and Doug would emerge in his blue striped pyjamas and take the breakfast tray back into the bedroom. We would hear them loudly reciting their morning prayers, wishing for a cure for coronavirus, thanking the Lord for our visit, giving thanks for their new house. We caught each other's eyes – grateful to witness such a long and lasting love. 'I want to be like Doug and Dulcie with you in fifty years,' you say. 'We will,' I reply.

Julian

It is 2015 and I have taken the day off work. The day is spent in a way that is familiar to me, with someone who skirts the margins. Julian lives in an aqua-coloured Art Deco apartment block opposite Bondi Beach. From outside his unit, you can smell the ocean. Julian is almost seventy. He walks slowly, with a hunched back, his head tipped permanently towards the ground, so top-heavy it is amazing that he can maintain his balance.

In my work life I am case managing thirty older adults in the community, many particularly vulnerable and living with chronic illness, some in extreme poverty. Everyone living complex and sometimes chaotic lives. Some are verging on homelessness, others are very confused and experiencing significant memory loss – getting lost for hours, giving away money to strangers, walking into traffic on busy roads believing they are on their way to work. People who are at crisis point. Some are experiencing elder abuse: financial, psychological and even physical abuse from those on whom they depend for their survival. A ninety-five-year-old woman was referred to us by police after she had crashed her sedan right into the window of her local IGA. When I first met her I knocked on her wide-open front door and she chirped a friendly hello. She wore an old frayed and dusty pink T-shirt nightie that loudly read I WOKE UP LIKE THIS. 'Do you worry about strangers or people who might be a bit suss coming into your home unannounced?' I asked her on my entry, to which she replied emphatically that there was 'absolutely no way in hell' she would ever let anyone in she didn't know.

Julian gets breathless easily, but when I suggest he slow down just for a minute, he screams 'Fuck off you cunt lesbian' in his usual high-pitched scathing tone. He has not washed in months, and his smell is a noxious combination of damp and cigarette smoke. His clothes are stained and hang off his skeletal frame. His fingers are yellow from decades of rolling his own cigarettes. Deep wrinkles line his brow, as if carved by a meticulous artist. Widow's peaks frame his once handsome face. His nose holds centre stage. He bends at gutters, collecting cigarette butts and under his breath mutters obscenities at passers-by. He picks up bags of trash from the street, gathers objects discarded, and carts it all home to his unit by the sea. People think Julian is homeless, roaming the Bondi streets talking to himself, spitting fresh combinations of homophobic or anti-Semitic insults. Those most familiar with Bondi know that Julian is not homeless but lives in the aqua Art Deco block by the sea. That he is the one with the sisters who care for him. Some cafe owners who have known Julian for years allow him to put out their tables and chairs of a morning, in exchange for a cup of coffee. He delivers the Fine FM music magazine as well as the local paper, slowly and steadily, a bag slung over rounded shoulders. When he cannot be bothered to do the rest, he throws what's left over a fence or hides them behind the local church.

Julian is my uncle. He is my mother's older brother. We are at the aqua Art Deco block by the sea because Julian's unit is a fire hazard. The block, for the second time now, is at risk of a $100,000 fine for Julian's consistent breaching of fire safety regulations. Julian's unit is cluttered and squalid. Inside, the floor is a sea of plastic bags, discarded bicycle pumps, a tent, broken furniture and many green Woolworths bags filled with figurines, candlesticks and clothes. There is mismatched Tupperware, a busted chair, pens and cigarette lighters, beer bottles, empty cans of tuna, a plastic bag with half a rotting roast chicken. His bathtub is occupied entirely by an enormous lion, carved out of stone. How it got there is a mystery. Lucky mice creep between his treasures and feast on food scraps that line the kitchen benches. The fridge is caked with black grime and the food inside is rotting. There are maggots. When opened it disgorges a smell of bitter earth and my eyes water. It is a sight and smell I know well and my response is a well-practised one. I close the door without expression, hold my breath, rise and move onto the next thing.

Julian has been ordered to clear out his home. He does not wish to be a part of this and doesn't believe there is a problem, despite the unit having no front door and the fact that each year he continues to have random people squatting inside. Julian claims they are his friends, until inevitably, they use or abuse him, steal his money, sell drugs from the front room, bash him up. His three sisters – two of whom have worked long lives as psychiatric nurses – have supported Julian for decades. His family of case managers assist by administering his money, left to them in trust by their mother – to ensure its safe keeping – so that it lasts Julian his whole life.

Julian is on the disability pension and cannot afford a fine. If the unit isn't cleared out, he will lose his home. When he was well, before schizophrenia overtook his life, Julian worked in the public service. His employer kept making up new roles for him – ones he could do, as his mental health and capacity for holding onto a functional life deteriorated slowly – demoting him year after year until he could no longer hold down any job. He used the money from his working life to buy his unit by the sea.

We are here, my mum and I, to clean out Julian's unit. We have hired Two Men and A Truck. Julian's pissed off. We spend hours working with him to farewell some of the clutter and when he is distracted, bags of rubbish get carted to the truck parked in the laneway. He is slow on his legs and so with every bag of rubbish that he tries to sneak back in, three more are taken outside. It is hard and stressful work, but with his cognition and capacity for insight damaged by years of drug and alcohol use, Julian cannot appreciate that this work is to maintain his independence, to keep him in his home. I tread this fine line at work all the time, balancing risk with trying to uphold people's autonomy, dignity and self-determination – though with family, the overstep feels easier in a way, yet it is still as heartbreaking. This is the best of a bunch of bad options. The worst being him losing his house by the sea and entering a nursing home in which he will curse out everyone until he is ostracised and completely alone.

The day we clear out much of Julian's stuff, we have arranged for an assessor from the local Aged Care Assessment Team to review him for aged care services for if and when he needs it. We are preparing for the crisis we know will come. If things get worse, Julian would have somewhere safe to go. The assessor is a composite of the people I work alongside – a social worker in a parallel team on the east side, supporting the same kinds of people I do in my job in the inner city. We know this situation well, Mum and I, though now the client is Julian and he's upset with us. Before the caseworker arrives, we have cleared out most of the main room and when she does, we offer her a crate to sit on. Our aim today is to declutter enough to avoid a fine, nothing more.

Julian will continue to collect and hoard; his mountains of kerbside treasure will accumulate until one day, two years later, he is found by police in his underwear, delirious by the beach, his legs purple to the mid calves, like socks, due to an accompanying and largely untreated chronic heart disease. He will never return to his squalid unit by the sea and will die in St Vincent's Hospital in a single room surrounded by bare white walls, a lone television hanging from the ceiling, and next to his bed a bedside cabinet on which sits a single vase filled with golden wattle. He never makes it to a nursing home, thankfully, not that it was ever his plan. His sisters are grateful for this fact. I'm in Olympia, Washington, on the US West Coast, when I receive the email from my mum letting me know that Julian has died.

At the beginning of the day when we arrived at the unit, we thought we were alone with Julian until half an hour into trying to allay him of his fears of the clean-up and convince him to let us assist, a groggy and dishevelled-looking man suddenly materialises from behind a mountain of junk in one of the bedrooms. His hair is wild, a wiry rim of red all around his face that connects to a beard long since trimmed. This surprise man is news to us, his rustling movements in my periphery the initial signs we weren't alone. Phil is someone Julian had met busking at Bondi Beach, singing Nirvana covers on his acoustic guitar. Phil appeared to have been sleeping on a large pile of clothes and bric-a-brac. He was initially combative, as if it were his home and we were encroaching on his private space. He and Julian had struck up an unlikely friendship and Phil appeared well schooled in the ins and outs of Julian's life. He was already aware of Julian's 'Three Evil Sisters', and quite accurately pin-pointed Mum as a key member. 'You're one of them!' he screeched. He had an enormous gap between his front teeth. He looked to be at least thirty years younger than Julian, someone clearly unwell and marginalised, too.

The Evil Sisters – as Julian liked to call his trio of siblings – worked tirelessly to support him, despite his verbal abuse of them. He would call my mum a fat cunt on each visit, tell her how terrible she was and how ugly she looked. That he might kill himself if he were that fat. They had roles, Antoinette and her sisters, Trude and Pat. Trude was the favourite, who left packets of ciggies and cash in the laundry basket of her Point Piper underground garage for Julian. He'd catch many buses to collect these gifts if he was running low. On childhood visits to Aunt Trude's, I remember long, hot afternoons of Julian drinking VBs in the sun, stinky and slumped on the sofa. He'd suddenly rise, slink out of the house and bus it back to Bondi.

Pat was the one who organised things, managed his finances, sorted out problems. She was pragmatic and blunt, indifferent and strong. It was on my aunt Pat that Julian relied most for logistics and when he got into trouble, since she was often the one who was most available. She saw him without fail at the same time every Wednesday. Julian's phone was so often broken or disconnected that eventually Telstra stopped fixing it. Julian and Pat had an analogue relationship. Same wall, same spot, same time, same day. If he didn't turn up, he was usually at one of the cafes that would still accept his 'help', or inching his way back home from the shops, stooped and slow.

My mum was the one Julian didn't like, for reasons that are complex, but are partly because of me, I think, because I am queer in an open and unapologetic way. What's more, Mum had also mostly done the hard and terrifying work with Julian in the past, when he was at his most floridly psychotic. Mum did deals with Julian, who hated hospitals and wanted to avoid them. The first time Julian was really unwell was the anniversary of their dad's death. He was religiously paranoid and fixated on good and evil, God and the Devil, sins of all kinds, possession. She told me she threatened Julian – giving him two options, that he stay with her and my dad for at least a week and trial psychiatric medication, or she would take him to hospital. Julian agreed and he stayed with my parents for a week. Mum took the week off work and during the second week, saw and medicated him each day. Years later, when he was once again increasingly paranoid and guarded, he must have remembered Mum had kept her word, for she threatened him again with the hospital. He acquiesced, allowing her to visit his unit by the sea every day for the next week. Despite never admitting him to hospital, and using her annual leave to do for free what she was often paid to do, Mum took on the bad sister role, took the hit of doing things Julian didn't like, copped the brunt of his insults. As she was already maligned in his mind, there was no point in the others getting involved. They all had roles to play.

The spite he dished out to Mum was anger misdirected. He was rightfully angry at what he did not get in his life. It was also a manifestation of his own internalised homophobia. For Julian, I discovered, was gay. His schizophrenia, his chaotic life and his poor mental health interrupted his ability to truly embody any kind of queer life.

I write about my uncle's mental illness as if it were only this that prevented his ability to truly embody himself in all his authenticity, or to participate in his own desired queer life, and fully enjoy it. As if mental illness does not have a context shaped by powerful systems and structures outside of him. The everyday language of the medical model, of psychiatry and psychology, is so individualistic that, as Vikki Reynolds reminds us, it masks the subjugating role that the helping professions have historically played. 'Helping professions' tend to construct people within a narrow remit, in pathologising ways, as traumatised, or addicted, or mentally ill, but often forget their location within a context that continues to manufacture and maintain everyday inequality via the larger systems of capitalism, which hinges on dispossession and colonisation. For her, my uncle Julian's mental illness, his drive to find relief via addiction, is inextricable from the ways in which narratives of homophobia and compulsory heterosexuality shaped the world he existed in.

Reynolds believes that superficial enquiry ends curiosity, especially when it comes to thinking about people who are mentally unwell. What this means is that if there is no curiosity, there is no space to appreciate how the mental suffering of many marginalised people like my uncle is linked to the systems of violence they encounter. We simply see a psychotic person, a person who looks dishevelled and drunk, whom we shift our gaze to avoid. Without curiosity, we don't take the time to peel back the layers to uncover and understand the structures that cause so much of these people's hurt.

My uncle's schizophrenia wasn't just a one-directional experience. His illness was created and maintained by structural forces that crushed him from many sides. When I think about Julian, I remember him as an individual who was unwell, but I feel angry at the ways in which structures made his life impossible. On one level, he was an unwell and disinhibited man cursing at the world, while on another, his life was stolen. His detour into drug and alcohol use makes sense in a world in which there was no room for him; his life criminalised, his humanity deemed second class.

Julian's disinhibition and rage is understandable to me when I cast a wider theoretical net. The contribution of psychiatry to people like my uncle was both to create, label and maintain his mental suffering, as well as shape the larger cultural discourse in which queer or mentally ill people were understood and pathologised. Psychiatry and psychology functioned in a kind of weird syncopation. They combined to developed a language of individual pathology, deployed to diagnose, ostracise and other, and in some cases criminalise people, while pedestalling particular forms of personhood. It values bodies and minds that are functional enough for work (i.e. not hallucinating or hearing things), and queer recreational fucking definitely was not consistent with acceptable personhood. Simultaneously, the unwell person was urged to trust that these same disciplines could help to heal themselves.

As a trans person living within a historical moment in which much has shifted in the field, it is interesting to note that this same pathologising still exists. There is still a system that asks queer and gender diverse people to surrender their bodies and selves to a bombardment of medical and psychiatric assessment in order to access medical care such as gender affirming hormones and surgery. While a more liberatory informed-consent model now exists in parts of the world, many people still must prove, often to a white, non-trans clinician who holds a significant amount of power, that somehow, our difference is worthy of help, that we should access the medical treatment we need. A difference that continues to be medicalised, othered and continues to feed a social and cultural story of people like me and people like Julian.

Julian's queerness came out more and more as he aged and became more disinhibited. There was a bit of a bodily and character softening. Perhaps this was in conjunction with a society that, in his lifetime grew more accepting of queer people. He started to speak in a higher pitch and with an inflection – like many of the incredible raging queers in my own life. He would often move his limbs in a more rubbery way, flicking his wrist, always with a cigarette in his hand, and quip something crude. He started to end many of his sentences with 'darling'. When he was in hospital, a few years before he died, he cursed my mum on her visit because she had failed to collect his pillowcase with his name embroidered on the front. He insisted all the nurses call him Jules. Years later, with more knowledge and curiosity of my own, it astonishes me that his authenticity escaped the cage of his own protective making.

I could appreciate the ire directed at his sisters in psychiatry, both incredibly smart, justice-seeking and strong women who are passionate and dedicated to work a lifetime in support alongside people whom society deemed too much, too unwell, too crazy. To Julian, they were part of the system that told him he was wrong, sick and aberrant. When he was later so unwell, why wouldn't he express such deep rage at them and the world? Why wouldn't he express a hatred for the faggoty niece who was hauling his scabby yet precious junk-shop treasure into the Two Men and a Truck's bright orange pick-up? It was on the backs of the trauma of people like Julian to whom I owed my queer millennial luck. The social and political shifts that queer and trans people have fought for and experienced in the decades since Julian was born is no more evident than the fact that, having left me some of his unit by the sea on his death, I bought, with my partner, our home in a small inner-city suburb in which our queer existence is mostly unremarkable.

My job in community social work was full of moments like the one in Julian's unit by the sea. It is a neat set of skills one acquires both in training and on the job – supporting and meeting people where they are at. The tools we have as community workers are in our bodies. We use our voice and words and appreciation for the ways in which systems create and maintain problems, we understand how they impact and shape bodies and people in life. We are aware of the complexity of power – and the contradictions in our own holding of it. We use tone to connect and maintain a sense of curiosity in all our interactions with clients. We have a capacity to hold complexity, to withhold and reflect on judgement, and underneath it all sits an awareness of the world's inherent inequity. It is in this territory of unfairness that we live and the motivation to see it shift helps us to seek justice for the people we support. We hold ourselves to account for the actions we do and do not take.

I told Phil about what was happening while Mum started cleaning up with and around Julian – who was swearing at her, cunt this cunt that. I told him that we loved Julian and that he was important to us, too. I took him for breakfast. This was mostly a tactic to ensure he was out of the way, one less distraction for us to deal with on a day that was already difficult for all of us. Phil told me that nobody had ever taken him to a cafe. He had never even had a coffee before. That such a small act of kindness had never been extended to him in his life was profoundly sad to me. He had a history like my uncle's. Phil struggled with addiction, homelessness, he had loose connections, was mostly without money and food. He lived a life on and off the streets. Sometimes, when he was drunk, he got into fights. That was how he lost his teeth, he told me.

When I was young, I remember being afraid of Julian. He was a dark and mysterious presence. He was long and lanky, dishevelled and did not talk to me very much. He was unlike anyone I had ever met before. He crept around the background of family gatherings, doing his own thing, often lying asleep on a couch as we gathered together to celebrate a birthday. He spoke slowly, as if half asleep and I remember his eyes were often half closed. He would show up unannounced at my nanna's fibro house that my grandfather and his friends had built, the one he and his four siblings grew up in, and take a bath. His childhood bedroom was out the back, and remained there for him, whenever he needed it. It sat off the kitchen and opened onto the patio, with its large collection of pot plants and climbing vines. Julian would stay with Nanna for days – quietly smoking and drinking and sleeping and taking baths. She would cook dinner and make lunches for them both and they sat in silence in the sun. He would while away time in her garden, pruning and planting and observing the changes of the seasons. Julian was more at ease when he was in the garden, as if he was most comfortable in communion with plants. I only later discovered how extensive his knowledge of plants and flowers was. When my nanna broke her wrist (gardening), she had to leave her home and move into residential care because she couldn't live alone anymore. She was eighty-nine. Julian planted her an entire garden out the front of her new room at the nursing home. He never came via the main security door; instead, Julian climbed around the back, entering via the garden that he tended sporadically. When she lost her sight, she could identify every flower via smell, with Julian describing to her all that she was missing.

My nanna gifted Julian his love of flowers. She passed on her knowledge and he was her keen student. She had a garden full of colour, flowers mostly, but I remember there were rows of strawberries in summer and a large and generous lemon tree. One day, goes the family tale, she discovered an unusual bright-green flowering herb with seven serrated leaves that she had never seen before. She took it to her botany club. 'What's this?' she asked them, oblivious. The next day, the police were on the doorstep to speak with Julian about his cannabis crop.

In the last year, I have quit my social work job and begun working as a counsellor. It was a long process, not only to build the confidence that I had the capacity to be a decent therapist, but also to prove I could meet the psychology centric standard that would enable me to bulk bill with Medicare.

I have most recently been drawn to a form of therapy known as Internal Family Systems (IFS). IFS is a model developed by family therapist Richard Schwartz in response to work he was doing with adolescents experiencing eating disorders.

Traditional ways of battling people's inner critics were back-firing, because the person continued to binge, or restrict their eating. His patients told him about their restrictive parts, and how they were in conflict with these other parts that wanted to get better. And so, Schwartz began to develop an inner family therapy model, loosely based on family therapy, that views and understands people as part of wider relational systems (i.e. families).

IFS sees individuals in much the same way, as having an inner system made up of multiple parts, a bunch of inner children, if you like. Inside me there is the people-pleasing part, the fear of failure part, the big achiever part, the over-functioning part, the responsible part, and there is the charismatic part. There is the justice-seeking part. There is the part that wants to be liked. In among them there is a part that often feels unlovable and not good enough. This part still shows up sometimes. The part that says, 'Erin, if you do good things, you'll be loveable.'

Not all parts are problematic, though we see these parts most in people who come to therapy. Most parts are normal aspects of who we are and they help us navigate the world, interact with our friends, make big decisions, experience pleasure. When there are competing voices in our head – say, the one that wants to eat the chocolate versus the one that shames you for wanting to eat it versus the one that urges you to do twenty laps of the pool to 'work it off' later – these are our many parts showing up.

IFS views self-harm, addiction, suicidality and various troubling behaviours, thoughts and feelings as communication from parts that have been wounded. IFS sees how these parts often take on extreme roles and responsibilities to keep the person safe, to help them avoid more pain. In IFS these parts are known as protectors, jumping in to prevent wounds being triggered. Troubling behaviours such as self-harm, reactivity, compulsive exercise, anger, addiction and anxiety are the work of parts engaged in the body's protective and adaptive strategies to avoid deeper pain.

Suicide in IFS is viewed as the ultimate protector, doing all it can to stop pain. It is a wild thought, to consider suicide in this way: not as personal failure or severe 'disorder', but as someone's last line of defence, the first responder responsible for ensuring the safety of the system and jumping into action. IFS contends that there are no bad parts and that if we are curious we can see all parts as having good intentions, even self-harm. Parts work is de-shaming.

For example, instead of exploring the effect of someone's drinking, or trying to get them to cut it out, both counsellor and client entertain a curiosity about the part of the person that drinks. What is it protecting? Why has it been forced into such an extreme role? How is it trying to help? What is the wound it's trying so hard to protect? The theory of IFS is that if we heal the wound that the part protects, then the part can find a new and more fulfilling job.

When our parts are working well together we access what Schwartz calls Self-Energy. When our protector parts take over, we blend with them and we have a harder time with life – we display symptoms, we are reactive, we self-harm. By using this model, we can hopefully separate ourselves from our experiences and have more compassion for ourselves and the parts that cause us pain. The aim is to move from being 'in' our experience to being 'with' it.

One of the big challenges in life is to be vulnerable with other people. With parts work, a lot of the parts are considered very young, often believing they are protecting someone who is still young, and not, as is the case most of the time, a grown-up person who can look after themselves. It's why when we are triggered, sometimes we act like a small child; we huff and puff and throw a tantrum. The part is young. The part that chronically avoids intimacy with others because they hold a deep sense of shame about who they are, is often someone who was relationally wounded as a young person – maybe by a shaming parent – or had an experience, like mine, of being bullied. We think if we get close to someone we'll be rejected. We forget that it's our nervous system talking, that the pain is old and our protective strategies are not necessarily needed in the current moment.

Frank Anderson is a psychiatrist who blends IFS into his work – a truly unusual mix. A training session of Frank's I attended had me thinking about Julian and also more about my own story; my own relational wounding. People carry so many narratives of who and what they are. They show up in therapy because they believe a certain story about themselves; maybe that they are bad at relationships, that they are a failure, an addict, that they're unlovable and hopeless.

Anderson believes that vulnerability is our superpower, but that for a lot of people, their vulnerability has been weaponised. To be vulnerable is to be who we truly are, to feel all our emotions, to align with our truth and to hold capacity for self-connection. Vulnerability is to take a risk and share it with someone else.[2]

Anderson points out that it is not our vulnerability that is the problem, but the reaction from other people to our vulnerability. It's not who we are that's wounding, but the reaction to who we are. When we show up, in all our vulnerability, especially as kids, and someone reacts to us in ways that hurt us, we internalise it. So the story we grow up with is that being vulnerable is bad, and that something about us is shameful. We grow into people who develop protective parts so that we don't re-experience the reactions that convinced us we weren't good enough. It is a violation of vulnerability, Anderson notes, that sees people's parts take on extreme protector roles, often doing all this work to hide our authentic and vulnerable qualities.

I thought about Julian's long-term schizophrenia, his long-term cannabis smoking, his alcoholism. Julian retreated into a world populated by few, and later it was mostly occupied by those who exploited him. I was curious about the extreme roles his parts were forced into, why they showed up in the ways they did, in his poor mental health. Where and how he had been hurt.

Julian, Mum remembers, was an effeminate, soft boy growing up. He was quiet and contemplative and later on, alternative and interesting – like a suburban James Dean: sulky and hot in his lanky, high-browed way. (He was also literally high-browed, a receding hairline being endemic to the men on Mum's side; something I have always found quite an attractive feature in my uncles. All their hairlines begin mid-scalp.) He was tall and mysterious, with an interest in fashion. He slicked his hair back and wore white shirts with leather jackets and jeans. He spent time in his room drawing and making art and even back then, he liked flowers and was interested in plants.

Mum recalls their father as a gruff and hard-working union guy. He was a nursing manager at Rozelle Hospital at Callan Park by the water, back then a large psychiatric hospital. He would ride his bicycle from Hunters Hill because even then, four kids in, they didn't have a car. Once a month he would come home from his weekend job at the bacon factory with a block of Cadbury chocolate, enough for everyone in the family to have three whole squares each. He had twice stood for Labor in the seat of Bennelong, the one John Howard famously lost in 2007, and when they did eventually get a car, on his one day off a month, he would drive the family to the Blue Mountains for a picnic.

He met my nanna at a Catholic dance in the 1940s when they were both in their thirties. They got together and wasted no time in making themselves a family of seven. Mum recalls her father as a man of few words who, at the dinner table, would grunt as opposed to speak. She recalls growing up, the second youngest, with her younger brother living with these 'old people' – their three elder siblings having already moved out of home. Their father would point at the salt shaker and make a noise, to which my mother would ask him to decipher his grunty Morse code. 'One grunt for salt and two for pepper, Dad?' she would ask, refusing to partake.

*

It's not surprising that an adult gay man like my uncle developed such extreme protective parts having been shamed by the adults in his life as a young boy because he demonstrated effeminate qualities, was different, liked to draw, was soft and considered. He internalised this shame and quelled his idiosyncrasies.

I imagined him growing up in a Catholic household in the 1950s and 1960s, in which queerness was seen as a sin, or at least something to be shied away from, to be ignored as a possibility. I imagined my grandfather, whom I never met, whose own protective parts were taking over (the part that didn't want a gay, effeminate son), and his reactive anger at Julian, his disappointment evident in derisive put-downs and in the non-verbal, the language of the household. I imagined the ways in which Julian's protective parts kicked in – his drinking, his smoking and later, the many voices in his head. I held onto sadness, knowing Julian was likely so burdened by his exiles, living so much of his life in hiding. Living a life mostly in the closet, attempting and failing to partake in a theatre of machismo, his queerness evident through cracks, his sense of self deeply wounded.

Viewing all this through an IFS lens, I too recognise how I internalised other people's reactions to me. I internalised my parents' unenthusiastic responses to my masculine leanings, the ways in which bullies at school tormented me. My vulnerability was not so much in disclosing stories about who and what I was, but in how I showed up, what I looked like, how I sounded, how I held myself in space. I developed my own family of protectors to ensure the wounds didn't sting me again, to prevent future hurt and shame. I grew my hair out, I once bought a G-string at Warriewood Kmart, I opted for a truly hideous dress at my high school formal. Once I even wore white pedal pushers with yellow trim and a Hawaiian shirt I tied in a bow at my midriff. Once I concocted an elaborate tale about a boyfriend in New Zealand. I worked tirelessly to hide the vulnerability that brought out painful reactions in others.

My aunt Trude, one of the Three Evil Sisters, died not long before Julian, within twelve months of receiving a Stage 4 ovarian cancer diagnosis. Mum reminded me of her late sister's support of Julian's intersecting identities: his Catholicism, which he tapped into as he aged, and his queerness. That together they would travel to Newtown to attend a church that embraced its queer community. They'd stay for tea after Mass, my aunt hopeful that Julian might find connection. He would go, though only if she picked him up. When I think back and remember Trude, bombastic, always with her camera out, often dressed in signature top-to-bottom white linen with open-toed bespoke sandals and red toenail polish, she simultaneously occupied two roles for Julian, that of big sister and fashionable and encouraging fag hag. Trude was the family photographer and in cleaning up her belongings, my mum and Pat had the task of going through mountains of photographs. Each time I showed up at Mum and Dad's, Mum would have a handful of photographs to show or to offload. One night, I arrive for dinner and she pulls out a photo of Julian.

In the photograph, Julian is wearing a bright, canary yellow T-shirt and on his head is a matching baseball cap.

There are other people in the photograph, friends maybe. Someone is holding a drink. Julian's face is wizened, a hard life already etched into it, but he is smiling, exuberantly. He is not beaming at the camera, behind which must be Trude, but at something or someone out of frame. I turn over the photograph, the back of which, in my aunt's distinct and beautiful handwriting, reads: 'Julian's first Mardi Gras – 1995'.

Periwinkle Blue

When you google image search 'shades of blue', tiles filled with all the blues appear across the screen. There is navy blue, cobalt, steel, spruce, electric, Persian, Oxford, ultramarine. There is berry blue, indigo and Egyptian blue. Sky blue. Azure, air force and bleu de France.

I was googling all the blues because there was a blue that sat, deftly, on the tip of my tongue. A blue I had forgotten. It was the colour of blue that covered the outside of the tiny terrace Merryn and I had just bought together. I was trying to write the letter we had long avoided writing. A note to tell our friends that we would not be getting married as we'd planned in November. The pandemic had halted that situation, for now. We knew it was impossible to have the kind of party we had dreamt about with our friends who were locked inside, their only holiday to a shop within five kilometres. The pandemic had shifted how we thought about how or what our wedding might look like and indeed even its centrality to us and our friends in a world that had turned ghastly overnight. Each weekend we'd promise to send out our note and each

Sunday would roll by without us having written anything. It was as if every weekend we pushed back against reality, staving off sadness, hoping our denial might fuel an alternate reality.

'What is the colour of our new house?' I asked Merryn.

'Periwinkle blue. Though it is often mistaken for lavender.'

'That's it.' I put it in our note. Told our favourite people that we'd not be getting married in summer but that we had poured our love and commitment to each other into a tiny periwinkle blue terrace.

There is a lot of privilege in both of these things – the getting married and buying a home. Many, myself included, appreciate that in a world that remains so unequal and unjust, these are not often at the top of queer people's lists of life dreams. Many are hesitant and have complicated feelings about participating in the theatrics of homo-normativity, particularly the desire to enter into an institution that long slammed the door in the faces of queer people.

As queers, despite the privilege we have as educated white people with stable work and families who have been support-ive of our queer lives, Merryn and I considered both of these things out of reach for a long time. So far out of reach they weren't even aspirations. For years, I perceived queers wanting to get married as apolitical and assimilationist. I was okay for the institution to be entered into and used to support continent-scattered lovers gain citizenry, yet I still opposed it for anyone else, out of dogged principle.

For many queer people I knew, gays entering into these dusty old dynamics were seen as diluting their own radical histories and solidifying a technology of social control. Buying into media hype that somehow marriage is the gateway to a meaningful life.

And here I am, still thinking with my complicated feelings about my own complicity. I don't believe my getting married neglects the complicated history of the institution, nor do I think my not getting married undercuts or dismisses wholly the struggles of queer and trans justice more generally.

We live in a deeply imperfect world. I held onto radical queer values because this was what I thought I needed to do. I hold them still, but in a less vice-like grip. I hold them with a sense of hope that disparate stances can sit together and the knowledge that I am imperfect. A living and messy contradiction.

It is an individual desire, in a world that remains still so virulently homophobic and transphobic, to want to have something that culture and society has long denied you, even if it's mythology. Even though I thought I didn't want it, I think, for many queer people, we internalise some of this – and deny ourselves the things (or even the idea of things, for maybe that's all it is) that might bring us joy. Things we can remake, re-story and repurpose.

Sure, marriage doesn't do much for unpicking the structural inequalities that infect queer and trans lives, but still I wanted to stand up in my finest outfit and tell my favourite people how much my partner means to me, how they have made my life profoundly joyful, and to commit to this life together as a team. So much of my existence has been about other people's comfort. It has been about blending in and not making too much noise.

*

I am making a home and this is what it looks like.

After the auction Merryn and their family and I walked in an elated daze up the street to have a coffee. I called my parents, put them on loudspeaker. 'We bought a house!' Yelps and congratulation burst through crackly reception. I left a message on my aunt's answering machine.

We drove Merryn's parents back across the Harbour Bridge, our nervous systems flooded with adrenaline. *What the actual fuck?!* We continued to look at each other in disbelief. Someone had died in a tragic head-on collision on the bridge just two days earlier. It felt almost unfair to be so happy, in the face of the losses of others. That someone's dreams and hopes had been dashed, lives instantly thrown into grief while our future simultaneously felt profoundly bright.

Driving home again, over the bridge to our rented apartment. 'What do we do now? We just bought a house!'

What do you even do? No appetite yet; our hearts were in our mouths. Merryn suggested we go home and fuck.

There's something nice about fucking when you know that it's been put on the list of plans for the day. You just know the fucking is going to happen. I appreciate these conversations when they happen, like on auction day, at least half an hour from home and in a very matter-of-fact way. Like talking about what's needed at the shops, or going to the gym. Later, soon enough, the plan is we are going to fuck each other. No fucking about, so to speak.

I nod at Merryn in the car in Harriet Street, Cremorne Point, and imagined the fucking that would happen later.

*

Once a week, we walk a small dog that belongs to a busy family. It is a job that brings both of us a lot of joy. The small dog's name is Fizzy and she is sometimes ignored at home by teenagers with more exciting things to do, her family working, schooling, forgetting her milling around their feet. So she comes with us in the car and we take her to all the parks we know. She is a beautiful sight, our Fizzy, who is part sausage dog, part kelpie. Many passers-by look at her quizzically, some getting it right, others merely stating the obvious: 'Oh, a big sausage dog!'

Fizzy is not one for balls, she just wants friends to run around with. She walks off the lead and doesn't run away and she turns back for reassurance when she runs a little too far as if to get permission to keep playing. Fizzy's favourite person is Merryn, something we share. When we pick her up and unlock the back fence, she writhes around in unadulterated ecstasy, jumping up and down, racing around in circles, trying to kiss our faces which are out of reach. Yelps of happiness come from deep inside her lumpy body and she is almost unable to contain her joy.

It was a Saturday when we bought the tiny periwinkle blue terrace. We had saved Fizzy for the afternoon, knowing she would be the salve our souls needed if we did not have the winning bid at the auction, which we thought might be our reality. She would be the perfect bookend to our day no matter what happened.

Because we had spent so long celebratory fucking, we had finally developed an appetite, and so, on the way to collect our weekly dog, we picked up felafel rolls. I wore my green raincoat with the warm fleecy insides and the enormous pockets. Winter was almost over, though the air was still crisp at four o'clock. Merryn drove and I spent the ride texting our favourite people the house news. We bought a house. On our laps we balanced the rolls, a crunchy oily mess of garlic sauce, pickles, tomato, olives and fresh deep-fried crispy green felafel, oil seeping through the wrapping in between desperate mouthfuls.

Pulling into Fizzy's driveway, we were greeted by the sound of her familiar yelps. We drove her to Sydney Park, the dog wonderland that was once an enormous city rubbish tip but is now one of the most beautiful city parks around. Our new periwinkle blue terrace is only a few streets walk from Sydney Park. We decided that we would like to see our new home and so once Fizzy has chased a few uninterested dogs around, we take ourselves there and just look at it. We find some friends on the way, whom we convince to come with us. 'We bought a house today!' we say. There it is with its SOLD sticker and its wonky front door, with the triangular gap at the top big enough for a piece of pizza to slide right through. Our friends are impressed and we imagine the life we will have inside there soon.

We stroll back through the streets of our new suburb and return to the old tip. We let Fizzy off the lead and she plays and comes back for reassurance and encouragement. Merryn gives this to Fizzy and she scuttles off again. We sit quietly on the edge of the park overlooking the city. Taking in one of the biggest days we have lived, a day where our commitment to doing life together has taken on new meaning. The sun sets and the air turns icy. We will be able to walk here soon, maybe with a dog of our own. Our future dog's name is Remy and we speak often about how much Remy will love it here in Sydney Park. Merryn says that it would be a crime against the dog community if we rescued a dog that did not like parks or other dogs. I agree. We take a selfie with the green grassy hill behind us as we watch the light fade over the city. We're beaming into the camera.

After we dropped Fizzy home, we stopped by my mum and dad's. Dad had bought a bottle of prosecco. Dad's love language is gift giving and he holds onto small bits of information, what you like, what you need. In this he shows his care in the best way he knows how. Once, when I worked at a video store in my first stint living out of home and was struggling to pay rent, I looked up at the next customer and there was Dad, hands full of groceries.

We popped the champas to celebrate the periwinkle blue terrace on the one-way street opposite the park, that we still cannot comprehend is ours. We toasted this big life achievement and re-told our auction story. How before the auction we'd asked the agent whether the owners might be willing to add the firepit into the contract and they did and now we have a house and a firepit.

We downed two glasses of bubbles and got to that sweet spot where the anxiety of family relating is dulled and feels a little easier. I don't know how we got onto the topic of hands, but we did. Mum's sister, my aunt Trude, who died a few years ago, had the most beautiful hands, Mum reckons.

She'd have them manicured and painted every week and on her deathbed in the palliative care unit in a Northern Sydney hospital, they were immaculate, painted bright red. Mum recounted a story about a hand model from the 50s who constantly wore gloves. She did nothing else in case she ruined them. No swimming, no washing dishes, no rock climbing. What a wasted life.

I was reminded of Nicole Kidman's strange clapping at the 2017 Oscars. Except she is not clapping really, she is slapping her palms together with her fingers outstretched, curving outwards as if her fingers were trying to escape their life attached to Nicole's hands. She is clapping as if she has flippers instead of hands. Clapping like a seal. Her hands inverted parentheses protecting 119 carats of diamonds, apparently. As with any good meme, when I plucked this memory from the crevices of my mind, it provided the most gratifying laugh. My parents had not seen this video. We pulled it up on YouTube and watched it many times over and fell about laughing.

We drove home. I didn't post a photo on the internet about how we had just bought a home. It felt too showy for the current moment. We will tell people in time, we thought, but not on Instagram. I post the photo of the two of us on the hill.

In the photograph, Merryn is on the left and I am on the right. We smile into the camera. Merryn's hair is wispy and tied back, though strands of it curl upwards and catch the last sunlight. Their hair is mostly silver now, grey strands interrupted by snowy rivers (and I never tell them this enough,

114

but I am so into it, that salt and pepper). Dimples pierce both of Merryn's cheeks and pull at the edges of a toothy smile. I am smiling, too. My face is crinkled at the mouth and at the eyes. My wrinkles are ripples in a pool, retreating into my cheeks. My mullet, untrimmed since the beginning of the pandemic, falls in barrel curls at my shoulders and the top sits flat and neat, as if a side part has asked the rest to walk in the other direction.

There is a lot of performativity in a selfie, though this photo lacks the orchestration usually reserved for the main page, which needs multiple takes for the perfect imperfect shot of a moment. In polyvagal theory, new understandings of the role the nervous system plays in shaping understandings of safety, and in turn, how people behave and react to their environment, there is a concept called 'neuroception'. It is the ways in which we, unconsciously, respond to cues of safety from within our bodies. It is a seeking out for who is safe, approachable. It is our eyes that do this work – and it is in the wrinkles of the eyes where this seeking out begins. It communicates not only that we feel safe, but that we are safe for other people. In diving into polyvagal theory, I have learnt more about the face. And it is with this new obsession that I look at this photograph of us on the hill in Sydney Park.

There is a genuine smile and there is a social smile. The genuine smile is also known as the 'Duchenne smile', after the nineteenth-century French physician Guillaume Duchenne who spent years studying facial expressions. In his smile, the eyes close, the cheeks move and the eyes crinkle at their edges.

The muscles that move the cheeks are called the zygomatic major and those that winkle the eyes, the orbicularis oculi. Ours are alive in this photo and they are dancing. We are sending cues far and wide that we are safe and we are home.

Routine

I have drifted to the comfort found in routine for as long as I can remember. When asked to describe myself, I would say I am rigid, a quality I felt some shame about for years. It was as if by mocking myself for my inflexibility, I was somehow reclaiming it. Currently awash in a pandemic that has quite literally enforced an unprecedented and regulated domesticity on us all, in which survival is found in the carving out of a life mostly indoors and isolated, I've come to think more flexibly about the role of routine, of structure.

My mum often reminds me of the moment when she really noticed my need for structure and routine. I was four years old. I remember this moment, too, though only vaguely. It is like a memory that comes only through the discovery of an old photograph. The story, like the photo, conjuring up a bodily memory I can see in tiny fragments.

I see it in flashes and colours. Mid-morning sun piercing through leafy eucalypts that tower over the playground I'm mucking around in, tucked into suburban bushland in the back of Sydney somewhere. I'm playing on multicoloured plastic play equipment. Woodchips cover the ground under-foot, to cushion falls from the monkey bars. There are other kids around me and I'm making friends, probably bossing them around. We're taken on a tour of the veggie garden and get to see how the composting toilet works.

'See that,' the teachers say, 'that whole house is made from recycled materials.'

I'm wearing a wide-brimmed hat; a hat I'd received from the open day at my local public school on the Lower North Shore. I'm almost in kindy and my parents have taken me to another school open day, a 'special school' they enthused from the front seats of Mum's Holden Gemini. The special school, I know now, was a Steiner school. I was a hyperactive, odd child, one they knew might (and did) have trouble in mainstream education. They thought my idiosyncrasies might be better accommodated in the flexibility of an alternative system – one focused on play and the uniqueness of the individual, and less concerned with success and competition. I don't remember much more than the feel of the playground wedged deep in the bush.

On the ride home, Mum asked me what I thought about the school. I'd liked it, though was unsure about the toilet. I asked about the uniform. There wasn't one. I was apparently immediately and immeasurably inconsolable at this news. No uniform! It was a wretched thought to me at four years old. I was unable to imagine a school without one. I could not possibly go there, I told her. And so I went to the school whose hat I'd already worn on the playground in the scrub.

*

My obsession with structure and routine may have also braided itself with my OCD, which for a long portion of my childhood took up a lot of space in my head and impacted a lot of the practicalities of life. Routine and order were somewhat obsessional, yet the order, the predictability of what would be happening and when, helped manage the obsessions. It seemed to soften the intrusive and pervasive thoughts that were so amplified without it. If the order was there, I could relax, get on with things.

Every school holiday, my dad would draw up a calendar for the period, each day's activity carefully pre-planned, decorated in his playful and colourful cartoon characters, some even with speech bubbles containing some encouraging holiday enthusiasms: 'Don't forget to slip slop slap!' said a wonky version of Roger Hargreaves's Little Miss Sunshine, who sported a towel over her shoulder on the Tuesday marked *Beach Day with After School Care*. Back then, scheduling was my parents' way of managing expected holiday anxiety.

Mum reminds me of another vignette, as evidence of my need for order, ritual – or perhaps, its role in moving us/me forward in a single day. It was my need, whenever we went out, to shopping centres especially, to immediately visit the facility's toilets. I like to think this was the nascent faggot in me, that the place fundamental to cruising was already endlessly fascinating. I would not allow us to do anything – no shopping, no fun – until we had found the bathroom. I would rarely have to go; I just needed to know it was there, to enter and have a poke around. I would push open the stall doors, turn the taps on and off and, once satisfied, I was ready for whatever else was in store, light and unencumbered. I'm not sure of the motivation for that bathroom obsession – though I like to think the end of the thread is found in the adult me, in the ways in which habit and predictability play in my days feeling more navigable. That there are events and rituals that I know will be there. If things turn to shit, so to speak, I know where to run.

It has been a consistent pattern, this need for aspects of life to remain more or less the same: patterns, numbers, activities. If the order shifted, chaos felt as if it were afoot. While the obsessiveness faded with age, the craving for the knowable and the ordered remained a consistent feature in my life.

Before the pandemic, I would exercise on the same days, at the same times, at the same place. I was not a spontaneous person and changes in plans were a real source of discomfort. Having bought a spin bike at the beginning of the pandemic, I went into the garage at those same times, on those same days, to pedal away in the dark. On the days I would have once gone to the gym, it would have been before work, and afterwards I'd stop for a coffee at the cafe next door. I looked forward to that coffee the night before – a treat I loved, which I would sip as I drove through the backstreets of Mascot, skirting the edges of the airport and Port Botany, through Rosebery on my way to my job at the jail. So, I recreated the routine as best I could, stopping by the same cafe, after my garage workout.

In her essay 'A Regular Choreography', Australian poet and essayist Fiona Wright recounts a trip to Iceland, exploring the narrative of travel and the flip side of travel or adventure, that of the homely, the domestic. The routine, the ordinary and how they tie into stitching together the days. She questions what it means, culturally, to travel, especially to someone for whom routine and ritual was so much a part of finding comfort and security:

> Travel is supposed to be transformative, worldly, independent, brave. It is supposed to be a breaking free from the things that bind us to our everyday and repetitious – and by implication stultifying – lives. We are supposed to value travel because of this, because it is international and not domestic, unsettling and not homely, disjunctive rather than routine.[3]

She notes that the rhetoric of travel is so often pitted against its opposite, that of the habitual and everyday. She goes on to note that the travel narrative:

> devalues everything that lies on the other side of the equation – the domestic, the homely, the repetitious and the known. The worlds in which we ground ourselves, locate ourselves, build the habits and small rituals that make us feel more comfortable, maybe even safe. The spaces where we may truly be ourselves – our private, unscrutinised and unperformed selves. Our small but significant selves.[4]

Wright considers two ideas about time, drawn from the work of Iris Marion Young and Simone de Beauvoir – the 'transcendent' and the 'immanent'. Wright affirms that we live our lives in both kinds of time – the first, being the transcendent, comprises big and important events, like travel, like love, like grief. Events and experiences that take us out of our regular day to day. Transcendent time, she says, are those 'moments where we are transported out of our regular selves and assumptions, where time feels different, slowed or furiously hastened; it is time that breaks the rules of everyday life'.[5]

Immanent time, is, Wright says, our home base. 'It is regular, unruffled, it passes mostly without us noticing.'[6] She explores the transcendent in the immanent habitual routines we make for ourselves, those often neglected as humdrum, domestic and safe. She describes her Icelandic recreations of small, everyday habits, rising early to write in a coffee shop, emailing friends of a night to round out the day. For Wright, these small acts were survival strategies – continuity, sameness, small pleasures of the knowable in the unknown. A way to better see the magic.

Hearing someone speak to these same thoughts and behaviours was comforting. Other people have a great fear of change and ruptures to routine, too! They struggle with the same dilemmas as me and hold tightly to trusted strategies to keep their bearings as well.

For a long time, I have been embarrassed by my rituals, or more precisely, by how fervently I cling to my routines. I know this used to be because I saw my repetitions as inflexibility, the same kind of pathological inflexibility I had been taught to recognise as part and parcel of my illness. It still makes me anxious to eat earlier than my regular meal times, to eat ingredients that aren't part of my usual repertoire – and these two things, at least, are inevitable when I travel. I still feel jittery and unsettled if I have to change plans quickly, have to rethink the regular patterning of my day. But I also know that when I'm doing well, it is routine and ritual that keep me on track, that keep me eating afternoon tea while reading in my favourite armchair, making supper even though I really do not want to, having breakfast while I write.[7]

It was in reading Wright's admission to feeling a sense of embarrassment about her rituals, her clinging to routine and struggle with travel that I experienced a sense of relief and detected hints of recognition. Whenever I have tried to push through my own immanent time – the one in which small and very organised rituals underpin a calm and knowable life, as I attempt to experience the transcendent and seek the rebellious adventurer inside – I have felt mostly ill-at-ease. In moments in which I have pushed myself – like almost moving to Olympia, Washington, before being kicked out of the US; or climbing up and sliding down Mount Agung, Indonesia's second highest mountain, in inappropriate shoes and a pair of jeans; or willingly being the third person on the back of a tiny scooter driven one-handed by a reckless man in a bright Hawaiian shirt who, while winding speedily through the tiny paved back streets of Nusa Lembongan, used the other hand to text on a flip phone – I found myself trying to cram the immanent into the transcendent.

In Bali, it was in the spoils of a fizzy drink, enjoyed over ice at sunset. It was paying the hotel next door an exorbitant fee to use the gym and buying a coffee afterwards. It was streaming *The Bachelor* in the hotel room. It was doing push-ups in the bathroom. It was in writing lists. Reading before bed. When stuck in Vancouver, awaiting the arrival of my lover for our final teary weekend, it was spending every afternoon at 4 pm in pigeon pose with Adriene of Yoga with Adriene YouTube fame in the dark basement suite of the punk house that took me in. It was in donning five layers of clothes and shuffling through the snow to Templeton Gym in East Vancouver, twice a week, to pay one Canadian dollar to use their tiny community gym. The room, a glass rectangle tacked onto the small indoor pool. On a good day, it could squeeze in about seven people. I'd take myself on international virtual hikes on the same model elliptical machines familiar from back home; Half Dome at Yosemite, Golden Cathedral Trail in Utah. Listen to the playlist on my headphones that I never bothered to change.

When I went to Berlin and took my first pill, I emerged from the dank club chrysalis, still wired, to a glorious sunrise and rode my cheap Mauerpark market bicycle to Melbourne Canteen in Neukölln to eat Vegemite and avocado on toast.

The image of the small me with the strong desire for a school uniform I connected to this larger story I carried around of being unadventurous and rigid. I saw it as proof that I had always struggled to be spontaneous, to try new things. It was shameful and embarrassing and I needed to be better at taking risks, at being more flexible. Now I can see it as my desperate need to fit in, and to feel safe, something aged four I felt I had to do because, even then, I knew there was something different about me. I wasn't like other girls, and a uniform brought me closer to them. There's also something else in it: a desire for order, sameness, regularity, predictability and structure. Every day, more or less the same.

Until COVID forced us all to confront the domestic, the small ways in which we hold together a life while living through a collective moment of trauma, I long problematised my incapacity for spontaneity. I did not hold much compassion for this quality. I hated on it, because it did sometimes get in the way of things. I was occasionally, like Wright, ashamed of how inflexible I was, and how unravelled I became in times of change. I feared it made me less interesting. When I was anticipating *Married at First Sight* on the telly one day and it was not on, I had a polyvagal meltdown, with safety and security found only in the watching of a *MasterChef* rerun. Close enough.

In thinking more about how the pandemic has us living in immanent time filled with small everyday rituals of routine existence, I have found a great deal of gratitude for the small ways in which my obsession with routine and ritual have anchored me throughout life. For how I have been able to tap into it during endless lockdown days. By being less critical of my lifelong aversion to risks, I've become more curious as to how that life got me here. COVID has provided a great deal of time to notice the habitual, the odd moments of rigidity essential to maintaining my mental health, and how they anchor me. How they are special and at times even funny. Once when I was dating several people, within a three-month period I took most of them to the same casual pasta restaurant because I loved sitting up at the bar, I liked the food and the comfort of the glasses they served the wine in. I knew what to expect. The waitstaff became friendly extras in my life. During the daylight hours, this back of Marrickville eatery became a cafe again; it was to here that almost every week without fail for the next six months, my partner and I would wander, order the same mushroom fried rice and hash browns, and complete the *Sydney Morning Herald*'s Saturday sudoku puzzle, falling in love.

I think my drive towards routine and ritual has been passed down to me over the generations by my family. I saw the aversion to travel, or to finding and making room for transcendent time as maybe an indication that we were scared, ordinary. I saw my own fear of change through this lens, too. Of course, travel and the capacity to do it is couched in both the narrative of travel as transcendent and worldly as well as the privilege of having time, itself something inextricably linked to the availability of funds to make it. Nevertheless, I saw my rigidity as boring and so I often hid these parts, navigated experiences in the world around the scaffolding of the banal and predictable. On our very first date, my partner invited me to play electronic darts in an inner-city basement. It was the day and time of my yin yoga class. I wrote back suggesting we eat some food after my class. I am incredibly grateful to this day that we made it to a second date.

I come from a white, middle-class family of non-travellers. I never went anywhere exciting beyond Tweed Heads to visit my grandma. We did not camp, we did not go on holidays. We once made a week-long visit to an inpatient psychiatric unit in suburban Sydney as a family, but this was no holiday. My mum and dad have not travelled much internationally, nor have they been to many cities in Australia, their lives lived mostly in the immanent. Dad went to Fiji once, Mum to Indonesia as a young activist and when I was four months old, in 1984, to a transactional analysis conference in San Francisco. (She once told me about endlessly pumping her breastmilk and feeding all the stray cats on the block, and I could only laugh.) My parents are well-educated, interesting, worldly people. Their idiosyncrasies no less significant for lack of the transcendent time associated with travel.

It does not appear to be something they regret nor something they have any desire for. Mum blames Dad for this reality. He never wanted to go on holidays and so she, married to him, didn't either. Mum recalls their honeymoon in Tasmania and how every morning Dad would play a round of golf. It is something he did every weekend – and still does. Apparently, before kids, when she suggested that they travel, she would encourage Dad by reminding him that he could find a golf course anywhere in the world, that he could inject his day with something familiar. His reply went something like: 'There are plenty here, why travel halfway across the world to do what I can do now?' He is an anxious man, I can see that – his transcendent moments are found in the habits intrinsic to the immanent time of his everyday. His anchor to the world is in reproducing the rhythm of routine. A way of existing I have inherited.

Dad's anchors are in his daily outing to his local bakery – the delight in the bleached white, crusty bread of no nutritional value, satisfying a hunger for routine more than anything else. I see it in his timed-to-the-minute walks with his eight-year-old rescue bull terrier, Ron, following the exact same route morning and evening. I see it vividly in his unflinching gym routine; the time and day and the reps devoted to each machine. I know this because for a short time we attended the same gym and he ended up, right there next to me, pedalling furiously in the corner on the upright bike. I remember feeling so affronted by his incapacity for change, by his inability to 'mix it up' for once so that he wasn't right there, in his floppy socks and his cargo pants. But of course, there was I, inflexibly the same.

Wright says that we have been taught that immanent time is the time of the ordinary and banal, a domain of chores and the unimportant aspects of the everyday. Immanent time has been gendered, she reminds us, because historically such tasks are the rituals of domestic and private experiences and have largely been those attended to by women. She argues for a refashioned relationship with the habitual and unspectacular so they become acts of anchoring ourselves to a semblance of normalcy, and a place where we find dignity and comfort. As qualities that nourish and sustain, to which we owe gratitude and curiosity. Sure, she continues, 'habits are homely, but it is for precisely this reason that they are important – because they allow us to rest, to dwell'.[8]

On her trip to Iceland, Wright observes Icelanders cohabiting with active volcanoes with a level of indifferent comfort. Their time is grounded in the ordinary pulses of small city life. What seems to fascinate Wright about the ordinary is 'that we stop seeing it, or at least, stop seeing it as remark-able when it becomes the stuff of our everyday lives'.[9]

When observed every day, the fact a city is wedged between glaciers and volcanoes that routinely means bridges collapse and roads require rebuilding, becomes less extraordinary. The landscape itself becomes immanent, just another facet of the everyday – its beauty only seen by the eyes of visitors passing through it as transcendent.

What does all this mean in the time of COVID? When transcendent time is so far away for so many and when isolation and the domestic – the immanent – is mostly all we have? Wright suggests that it is in paying attention to where transcendence can be found, glimmering in the ordinary. Just as the ritualistic, immanent markers of everyday city life allow Icelanders to live so amiably alongside their active volcanoes in all their destructive unpredictability, the grounding rituals of the most unspectacular domestic routines we cling to during the pandemic are our own quite remarkable survival strategies. COVID is our active volcano, simmering along just as violently underfoot.

I have a weekly planner. It is set out Monday to Sunday across the length of an A4 landscape page. I print it out each week, write the plan for each day, then tuck it inside my diary, which itself holds seven days to a double page. Sometimes the diary doesn't have room for the minute details of things that I have planned or the estimated time frame in which they might happen. The diary is a precis while the planner is an opportunity to flesh out the detail. There is not a significant amount of variation to the weeks right now, yet the planner itself is part of the ritual. I sit with it under the orange lamp on the golden, velvety couch in the living room on a Sunday night, pencilling in: ride bicycle, work, take Remy to the park, write, make granola, roast cauliflower for dinner, pack work lunch. None of these things I would forget if I did not write them down, yet it is comforting to see them written down, in their place. It feels grounding and intentional. *What am I doing with my days?*

The writer Annie Dillard reminds the reader that 'A schedule defends from chaos and whim. It is a net for catching days.'[10] Like Wright, Dillard sees small habits of the everyday help to craft a sense of order threatened by catastrophe. Our small habits are our own idiosyncratic methods of surviving within a life that can be chaotic and full of noise. A way to convince ourselves that our days make sense. For Dillard, a schedule musters the small pockets of time and what we do with them and are:

> a mock-up of reason and order – willed, faked, and so brought into being; it is a peace and a haven set into the wreck of time; it is a lifeboat on which you find yourself, decades later, still living.[11]

Immanent time, as Wright so beautifully noticed, is this regular choreography, something to help us function fully. The grounding, homely rituals are those that can help us participate in the transcendent, where and when we find it. She wrote her essay two years before the pandemic forced us into living a repetitive, domestic present. Who could have imagined a world in which global and domestic travel was impossible, one in which visiting friends or family held such deadly danger.

To imagine the very scaffolding of lives cordoned off, shut down apart from the most basic aspects of existence. Everything diluted down to the 'essentials'. If the pandemic has taught us anything, however, it is that essential is far from ordinary.

So much of Wright's work interrogates the small moments of daily experience, particularly ideas of home, stability and rootedness. What is it that connects us to a place and to a life? Wright's chronic illness means she is attuned to the familiar, averse to too much risk, for it is in the body one must find a home and safety, too.

> Standing still, or moving in repeated tiny orbits – this is how we connect with, and cope with, the much more ordinary existence that really is the stuff of so much of our lives; and our habits are how we attend to it, pattern over it and shape it – unspectacularly, perhaps, but beautifully, gently, and in a continual and immanent present.[12]

The world as refashioned by a pandemic has provided me the space and time to see and think more fondly of the habitual and rigid qualities of both my personality and my life that I've often found irritating and others have found difficult (sorry about the darts, my love). I can see my own tiny orbits in new ways; as mechanisms that hold together a life. My emotional survival has simply dropped anchor in activities most reachable; the knowable, predictable and small.

The pandemic has allowed so many of us to view and develop our rituals and routines. To notice in these small daily repetitions how they help us manage, what they say about what we are good at, what it is that we value, and what might need to change. It has highlighted what is close by and maybe, too, what matters.

I realise that one of the things that matters is the role of the ordinary, the small, the habitual in keeping me alive, and hopeful. I have been grateful to notice the peculiarities that underpin my days, to finally view them as nourishing.

I am nourished by the granola I make each week out of nuts and peanut butter and coconut oil that sits in an old one-kilo kalamata olive jar with a red lid. I fold the pecans and the walnuts and the sunflower seeds and the coconut flakes into the salad bowl then I warm up the peanut butter and the oil and I pour it over the top. I mix it all together with my hands and I pour it onto the non-stick baking dish that dear friends bought us for our housewarming and, a year later still has not one scratch on it. I bake it and then it sits on the top of the stove while it cools. I eat it with coconut yoghurt in the same spot on the front couch, looking out into the trees in the park opposite my house and with it I drink a coffee that I make with a splash of oat milk that counters the bitterness. I think about this breakfast the night before and when it is over, I am grateful it is a ritual I can practise again and again. I am nourished too by the medium-sized dog who sits as close as possible to me as she can, as I tap away, with her golden fur and her brown eyes framed by bronze eyelashes. The same walk to the park, her trotting ahead, me in the same grotty grey hoody, pockets full of treats. Treats doled out to her kerbside, when she stops and sticks with me, the boss. At the sandy dog park, I walk laps of the perimeter winding in and out of trees, sunlight flitting through them, listening to the same podcast, transported to the same place while the golden dog speeds figure eights around the park, somersaulting and wrestling with her friends. Sometimes taking a moment to sit quietly in a hole she has dug herself into, her enormous tongue, almost pornographically flapping as she rests. The walk home, her tired, muscly body pacing slowly by my side. We wander back into the house and I feed her. I put the kettle on, make the black coffee with the AeroPress and drink it out of the ceramic green mug that has been made by someone's hands and has added a tiny joy to this everyday ritual. I carry it outside to the room where I write and I put it down next to the laptop. I open it, ready to begin.

The shame long attached to the narrative of my own rigidity and routine – that it's dull, ordinary, dreary and not very queer – has been displaced courtesy of a traumatic global moment. Being in lockdown, trucking away at a life that has been stripped bare of connection, company, conversation, activities of ordinary life – has me looking at routine and rituals in new ways. I marvel at my industriousness in getting my spin bike; recreating a gym routine; how I could assert my boundaries at the swimming pool in years past, insisting my friend Amy not talk to me before we do our thirty laps of the pool. I want to continue to reject old stories that I am unadventurous or boring. The domestic is where I live and this is just fine. I fear planes and travel and change, I like to know what is for breakfast before the end of dinner. The small and the routine are important to me and I have more space to listen. Anxiety for me is lessened by the comforts found in the ordinary and it does not need to be pitted against others' capacity for a more easy experiencing of transcendent time; people like my partner, who has jumped out of a plane, skateboarded, lived in several states including in a house with no front door in the middle of the desert without electricity and who, with a level of nonchalance sat between that maniac on the scooter in Bali with his flip phone texting and me, sobbing and hyperventilating behind, certain that death was upon us.

Big Sue

The night I met Big Sue I was in my Steve Jobs get-up: black jeans, black skivvy and bright, white sneakers. I had successfully grown out a mullet and had half of it in a topknot, the rest a mess of curls cascading down my back. On the way to the bar, I wore an oversized black puffer jacket that I had found hidden in the back of my wardrobe. Bought a year ago, tags still attached. Apparently, they were in fashion now, puffer jackets. So, I put it on.

Big Sue came up to where I was sitting, next to a kaleidoscopic grazing plate of barely touched treasures including these delicious miniature pickled onions that both Big Sue and I appreciated with an equal, unadulterated zeal.

I had not expected to meet someone like Big Sue on this night out. I was dressed in my best skivvy because I was meeting, for the first time, Merryn's workmates. It was the boss's fiftieth. The boss was a fierce, genderqueer public health nurse whom everyone had so much time for. I had heard about these people for years, this team of health workers who were like family to each other, who spent their days together immersed in the world of sexual health. I imagined them as if they were characters in a novel, albeit with special skills in differentiating chlamydia from gonorrhoea. All with a dexterity for talking candidly about sex, for lancing cysts, freezing warts off genitals. Most of them were queers and weirdos, freaks – my kind of kin. I was excited to meet the characters who populated my beloved's life away from ours.

It is a sacred space, that of other people's work lives. So often, we can only imagine what that world looks like, mainly because we are too busy living out our own parallel working life, inhabited by its own cast of misfits. And so I was lucky at the fiftieth, as it gifted me the opportunity to visit.

Big Sue, I later found out, was an old friend of the person whose birthday we were celebrating. She wore an oversized, faded red T-shirt, blue denim jeans and boots. She had greying hair pulled back tight in a ponytail. Her face, animated with stories. She was solid and strong and stood six foot tall. Her voice, loud and deep and earthy. Big Sue held an energy that belied her age, which was sixty. She carried herself chest-high, like a jolly Viking, and defied the categories of age and gender just in the way she stood.

Big Sue zeroed in on me at the grazing platter and stared at me intensely with a look of amazement and disbelief on her face. She didn't need to say any words, the awe sat in the upward curve of her grizzled brow. It was as if my existence baffled her, and she kept gazing with a breathless, speechless glee, looking at Merryn next to me, then pointing to me, as if to say, 'Can you believe this guy?'

In these moments I brace for when people open their mouths and for something transphobic or ignorant to spill out, as they struggle to categorise and contain. I was thinking to myself, as I scoffed baby onions, *Jesus Christ, maybe Big Sue's a TERF and is going to give me shit about my moustache,* of which, recently dyed, I was very proud and saw as a great ensemble item.

Big Sue convinced me in those first few moments that maybe she belonged in the doghouse, but what she lacked in language she made up for quickly, first asking if I was a trans-sexual and then commenting that she loved my moustache. She looked at me in a constant state of astonishment. Initially I think she thought I was in dress-ups, as if she couldn't quite believe I might always live my life this way, always hard to pin down. We clarified that this was where I lived and she remained enthralled the whole night, both by the pickled baby onions to which we repeatedly returned, and the moustache. She also spent a lot of time complimenting my teeth – again, strange, but it was wild to be experiencing this kind of appreciation from someone. My body is mostly the source of curiosity in public spaces unless explicitly queer, where I am at home and understood.

Big Sue was actually about to leave the party when she first spotted us by the grazing platter, but then she became too invested and excited to leave and told me she would stay because she wanted to spend time talking with me. This mainly meant Big Sue talking at me about her many lives working on farms and in factories, recreating how she manoeuvred her bulk to lift heavy barrels on farm jobs, where she worked almost exclusively among men. She recalled all the ways she'd never fitted into anything gendered, and didn't see herself as a woman, either. She told me that 'Whoever can do the job best should do the job' and lacked the more nuanced critique of power that plays into these kinds of meritocracy arguments these days. Big Sue was, at times, very close to verging on slightly problematic-misogynist-dad, but she was enthralling. I was curious and I asked questions. She was, unbeknown to her, giving me one of the more affirming moments of my recent life, one in which I was constantly pushing away gender. Each binary – male, female – like opposing walls, trying to crush me as I stood solid and tall between them, skivvy sleeves up and my palms braced against each wall, holding them agape.

Big Sue held a schooner permanently aloft and sometimes she would shove it in my direction, beer sloshing about, and nod her head as if she was cheers-ing the moustache, and without words she'd just smile, having a moment to herself. She told me she loved how I was 'fucking people up', and was so energised that she stood about guffawing and toasting her schooner towards my face. Big Sue kept apologising to my partner for 'stealing' me away, as if she were an intruder on *Love Island*, wanting to know more, gravitating to her newfound crush. I don't think this was quite it; rather, it was more the case of an affinity, an unspoken experience of sameness and solidarity. Perhaps I was a visible representation of her experience, that of never quite fitting in.

I hadn't felt this special in so long. I was a curiosity Big Sue had stumbled across on her travels; a kindred non-binary spirit. I filled her with a childlike curiosity, and she me. I ached to understand how she had defied the structures from which I was only now, twenty-five years her junior, finally finding liberation.

I imagined Big Sue as a competitor on the television show *Survivor*, careening through one of those challenges where you bust through wall after wall made of woven-together sticks of bamboo until you come out the other side. Except Big Sue was lightly smacking them out of the way with a sense of dogged and comfortable ease. In my mind I see her majestically gliding past them, like a swimmer carving through water. I imagine this is Big Sue in life; all the time there she is, waltzing through the sticks, never getting scratched. Living her bold and unapologetic life.

Love Story

The last time I saw her, properly, in the context of an 'us', she was sitting on a rickety garden chair, amid the unkempt, overgrown grass of the backyard of the share house she lived in with two other women, both with blazing red hair. She was tapping at her laptop, a cup of black coffee steaming on the rusty cast-iron table beside her. Early morning sun filtered through lofty trees, illuminating the still-dewy grass. She was editing the weekly email newsletter for the volunteer-run radio station she worked at – 'Due by twelve,' she muttered, without looking up. She was wearing a red monochrome tracksuit, and the thick, brown hair of her pixie cut was still ruffled by sleep.

She and her flatmates with the blazing red hair called it the sunken house because it sat at the foot of a steep hill, and from the road you could only see its roof, as if it had been swallowed by the earth. Only if you peeked over the front fence could you see there was actually a house there. Getting to the front door required dexterous footwork. The backyard extended the length of the public park next door, the trees forming a canopy under which many independent bands would play while tote-bag-toting hipsters would sit with longnecks in their laps, nodding silently to indie folk and experimental noise.

When I was first falling in love with her, I baked vegan pumpkin scones for a party at the sunken house in an attempt to impress, and bumped into a famous musician on the front steps. I remember a feeling of overwhelm; a person with such social ties might want to have sex with me.

We'd had a literate passion via Myspace messages and splitting a ten-ticket pass to the Sydney Film Festival. My initial infatuation with her had been ignited by my ex-partner's long-time listenership to her late-night indie music radio show, *Unputdownable*. The show's title was both retrospectively ironic and a fitting description of the strength of feelings I held for her over the next decade. Our eventual, short-lived romance, given its complicated origins, was perhaps doomed from the start.

She dumped me from Barcelona via Skype while on a month-long holiday, travelling to a range of countries where she could practise her Spanish. I emailed her, asking whether she might want to wait until she got home to make such a decision. She emailed me back: 'I want to have kids before I'm thirty and I know that it's not going to be with you.'

Our time, from memory, was spent mostly fucking in the doorless loft bedroom of her mum's house that was accessible by a staircase off the loungeroom. The room was divided by a floor-to-ceiling bookcase that brimmed with hundreds of CDs, records and books. Whole days were spent eye-gazing and listening to Mazzy Star and going to experimental music shows. It was the biggest love I'd known. I was quite comfort-able, at that point, in my queerness and presented in life as a faggoty dyke. She was, ostensibly, a straight woman and I could tell that something was happening for her. When we went out to events, I could sense her unease when with me in public spaces. I felt it as rejection, another indicator of not quite being good enough, while she, perhaps, was plagued by fears of being seen as not quite straight enough. We would fuck creatively under a bridge in my tiny three-door Hyundai Getz, and then, upon parking outside her house, she wouldn't invite me inside. I'd drive home, wretchedly, over the Anzac Bridge. I ignored most of the signs of unhappiness and unful-fillment, and filtered out all the ways her own shame seemed to get in the way of letting me in.

She introduced me to music I had never known: Electrelane, Beach House and Love of Diagrams. She scored us free tickets to The Cure at the Sydney Entertainment Centre. We saw big international touring bands and went to noise shows in crumbling warehouses. She wore vegan boots and tunics with white button-ups underneath. She once told me she had to spray Rescue Remedy under her tongue before one of our dates because she was so nervous. She introduced to me her then all-time favourite band, Yo La Tengo, one I still consider among mine. Together we discovered Arthur Russell, Panda Bear, Grouper. She might have been in denial about the parts of herself that were queer but she held a soft spot for Vancouver-based post-punk band The Organ. The band had featured on the lesbian television series *The L Word*, a show that happened to be the highlight of my late adolescence and whose climax coincided with my own coming out. She interviewed them on her radio show and wrote about it for a music magazine long lost to the internet.

If people in her life did something she didn't like she cut them off. I had, via our short time together, acquired friends of my own through her, some fellow tenants of the sunken house, some guests – most of whom still remain peripheral people in my life. None of those people see her much anymore, an experience I share. A cutting off. A moving on.

The night before she sat in the morning sun in the overgrown grass in the monochrome red tracksuit, she had texted me: 'I miss you, will you come over to the sunken house?' She had returned from Barcelona some weeks earlier. I had spent these weeks tending to my broken heart with an array of Aldi treats I couldn't finish, and by crying a lot.

Against my better judgement, I drove over to the sunken house. It was late on a dark, quiet weeknight. She opened the front door and I slipped inside. We didn't speak much. I remember her room to the right of the front door, dimly lit by lamplight, her sheets made from the T-shirt material that is an ideal springtime bedding option, right there, a perfect middle ground between flannelette and cotton. I remember her nakedness on top of me, her large brown eyes tethered to mine. 'I love you,' she said to me, clearly. I returned these words and we slept.

The next morning, I woke to find her in the garden in the early sunshine with the laptop among the dewy, sunny, overgrown grass. The monochrome red tracksuit. Eyes that wouldn't meet mine. I didn't know what to do. I felt tiny, sensing my presence as only a nuisance to her. I said goodbye and silently slunk away. Confused, but hopeful that her 'I love you' indicated that our lives might merge again.

Our lives never merged again.

For the next five years my heart would sink at the sight of her. She'd offer me a kind gaze, silent hellos at shows or ignore me altogether. I knew when she was in a room even if I couldn't see her. I continued to punish myself, listening to her radio show late into the night. Her idiosyncratic voice, so curious and kind, always straddling the edge of a chuckle. I would think to myself, *That was the voice that once said 'I love you'*. One night, driving home, I was stopped at the intersection of Canterbury and Old Canterbury Road near the McDonald's when I heard Joanna Newsom's 'Erin' come on the radio. Newsom's sad lyrics were, to me then, some kind of message. They were probably not, but in heartbreak we read much into the behaviour of those who once loved us. We did not yet have Instagram and so it was in radio-show listening and blog-reading where I searched for meaning. On reflection, it is quite the bold move to play a song with a title that shares your ex's name and not have them, as it had me, believe it might be attempting to say something. Regardless, I was listening for subliminal messages across Sydney's independent radio airwaves.

My ears felt hot at the first lines – the repeated declamation of my name, the enquiry if I could hear the song for me. My heart broke at the fifth, sixth and seventh verses, at the mention of Shenandoah, of life being sweet.

I took it as an offering that I was important to her. That despite everything, she was still thinking of me. Maybe she did love me, even if all she could ever do about it was to play a song called 'Erin' on her radio show.

I played that song and cried a lot. I tried to dissect its meaning. I analysed it, bereft but hopeful to find meaning and understanding where there was none. I googled the lyrics many times over. I typed in 'What is the meaning of Joanna Newsom's "Erin"?' and 'Is Joanna Newsom's "Erin" a love song?' I discovered that Shenandoah is a Native American word for the ways stars sparkle on the water when viewed from a mountain range. That it loosely translated to 'clear daughter of the stars'. It felt like the conversation I needed. The one she couldn't have. I don't really know, for I live only in my skin. To her, our connection may have been so fleeting to have been altogether not very important.

I thought about her often for many years, wondering whether there would ever again be a fire in my belly so all encompassing. Three years later I went to an art show on Cockatoo Island. I glimpsed her from my place in a long line of people waiting for tickets. She was heavily pregnant, mere days away from the first of two babies she would have before thirty. She looked majestic in her ballooning tunic and my heart dipped a little less. I was unable to imagine that life anymore, but seeing her, removed yet so familiar, was a gentle reminder that there was a piece of lifetime that was ours alone.

More years later and I see her at another art show. We are both in our late twenties now. We are sitting side by side together on the floor, waiting for the show to begin. It is the first time we have spoken since the morning in the grass. Her youngest child has a cute name, much like the eldest whose middle name is that of a summer stone fruit. I say 'Congratulations on your new baby' and we exchange a snapshot of our lives. She asks how I am and I say that I am good and that it is nice to see her. Her voice has the same soft, gentle charm and her face crinkles in its usual places and her movements are ones I remember well. We know so intimately the sounds, the walk, the ways of the body. My love comes back instantly but it lives in a new place now. It is a fondness for memory, not a wish to return.

More years pass and I walk past her at Broadway Shopping Centre. I sense her before I see her, briefly, and soon we are on our way again. My heart skips a beat. It is brief and welcome.

Some ten years later, in the year of Trump's election I was dating an American who was in Australia for a holiday but whose hometown was Olympia, Washington, the birthplace of Riot Grrrl. The Pacific Northwest was the home of Bikini Kill and Bratmobile and so many of the musicians we listened to in the loft bedroom without a door. I wanted to tell her about this new life of mine, especially when I decided to move there to be with my anarchist girlfriend. 'I'm in this historical music place,' I wanted to say, 'Kathleen Hanna sang at this bar I am drinking at in the 1990s. This tiny, quaint, radical town is the birthplace of the music that means so much to you. I'm living with these queer freaks and I'm going to punk shows and it's great.'

For a brief moment it *was* great. A few weeks into my more permanent move, after a weekend away in Canada, I was detained at the US border, taken in for questioning and denied re-entry to the States. My relationship was instantly shattered. I remained in Vancouver, devasted, broken-hearted, deciding what to do.

I fell in with what felt like the Canadian equivalent of my Sydney queer family – punks who mostly worked in social justice jobs, played music, went to shows. A failed sublet with a butch Australian astrologer found me in the punk-house basement room of a holidaying nurse. Their room felt like the amalgamation of the rooms of every queer person I had ever known. I cried with a deep gratitude to find myself among such decent people who took in friends of friends when they were having a hard time, because this is what queers do.

The books and the posters and the art on the wall was familiar and comforting. DIY punk show posters, fundraiser flyers, an old but working record player. The Collective Tarot. Marx. There was one of Australian artist TextaQueen's illustrations on the wall looking down over me. Jeanette Winterson sat on the bookshelf alongside *The Ethical Slut*, Alison Bechdel's *Dykes to Watch Out For*, Butler's *Gender Trouble* and half of the queer canon. I noticed the set of Knausgaard and I was glad to know other queers also have a contentious relationship with introspective literary autofiction. My basement room had its own ensuite with a pink enamel bathtub into which I slunk and cried and tried not to get my (borrowed) books wet. One night, I noticed that there was a pillowcase with the face of Britney Spears hidden under the bigger ones on the nurse's bed so that when I went to sleep I got a surprise. I spent time with Adriene who is many people's online yoga friend – doing downward facing dogs and savasana. I felt that, by the end of the sublet, she and I were good friends and when

I remember my time in Vancouver, Adriene feels like just one of the punks who supported me. I promised myself I would never google her or look at her Instagram so as to not spoil the illusion that she was solely *my* friend.

I had decided to stay in town another week, to wait for my girlfriend to drive up from Olympia for one last tearful weekend together. And so when the holidaying nurse returned, I needed another place to stay. The housemates upstairs organised some farewell drinks for me. Despite my doldrums, I had been quite the guest, apparently. They told me they'd miss me. They called me The Australian and I was offered a room by another queer woman. She had a small, yappy terrier called Bruce, named after Bruce Springsteen. It was only on the day of the move that she told me she was a musician. She said she wasn't playing much anymore but was once the drummer for The Organ.

I asked her whether she remembered her tour of Australia years earlier, the interview with the woman with the big brown eyes and the tunic and the soft caramelly chuckle from the small community radio station in Sydney. She did and, in this moment, I felt the world shrink. In Vancouver, readying myself for my next big heartbreak, I was intercepted by the collision of past and present. It was the gentle reminder I needed: that maybe, one day, years from this moment, I'll see this lost connection as a real gift, too.

Risk

Merryn took up ocean swimming in September. Their dad has been swimming at and returning from Balmoral Beach for almost two years now, having given up the local chlorinated hot box that sat atop a building that was his local pool. He found a crew of early-rising beach swimmers, never looked back.

I am petrified of sharks. Well, the idea of sharks, I come to realise, when I interrogate why I cannot ocean swim, too. Everyone, my partner tells me, is likely petrified of sharks. Those who swim in the ocean probably just think about risk differently. In statistics. In what is gained by leaning into risk.

I was having a bath outside in the clawfoot bathtub we have wedged between the wall of our tiny house and next door's fence. It sits flush against the sides so you have to get into it from the front and try not to tip it over and when safely inside you can look up and see the sky. There's no room inside our place for anything, let alone a bathtub. Merryn's voice comes from beyond the bathroom window above my head. 'Remember when I first went ocean swimming and we talked about the risks of doing things, that it began as a bit of an argument?'

I had completely forgotten. I am in the middle of editing my manuscript and remind myself that I need to include this episode. It's integral to the story.

We disagree about the ocean initially. I don't want Merryn to die and, essentially, I don't want Merryn to ocean swim. I project my fear of sharks and danger. I catastrophise and I ask why they would intentionally, by ocean swimming, place themselves one step closer to death when they could make different/safer/less risky choices, like swimming in the ocean pool. I was rigid. I likened it to bungee jumping or plunging thousands of metres by skydiving out of a plane – both to me, just an express lane to death. As if those activities could quite easily be cut from someone's life and an accident avoided altogether. My rationale at that point, fuelled by killjoy fear was, if you can make solid choices that enhance your ability to stay alive, why not?

For Merryn, swimming in the ocean was enjoyable, a risk worth taking. A risk that came with the reward of awe and wonder and accomplishment. An antidote to a full-time work week in nursing, itself a place that holds large amounts of risk, especially in times of rapidly spreading COVID-19. We talk about how the unknown somehow feels riskier, maybe for that very reason, since we are so unfamiliar with it. However, we forget how many of our daily activities are inherently deathly because they are so known and so ordinary. Others we have just adjusted to because in taking some of those risks, our lives are more worth living.

Merryn gets out their phone: 'Statistically, driving to the beach is more lethal than any beach-related dying.' I look up the statistics on surgery. If I have top surgery, the risk of dying from complications is also far greater than a shark taking a bite.

Merryn signs up for a three-weekend ocean swimming introductory course with a friend from work and a bunch of other risk-taking sun-kissed Bondi locals. I drop them at Bondi Beach each Saturday and because I also love swimming but am too anxious to join them in the open water, I drive the twenty minutes in traffic to Wylie's Baths, the 46-metre ocean pool in Coogee, to do my laps in relative safety. A drive, I realise once I get there, that carries with it a far greater risk than Merryn's dip in the sea. On the return trip to pick them up, I'm more attentive as I wind back through the snaking streets of Coogee, Clovelly, Waverley, Bronte – to find Merryn and the swimmers at a bookstore cafe, eyes twinkling: this is it, a new love is beginning.

I watch Merryn's love of the ocean unfurl. I am inspired by their bravery, panicked at the thought of them ever being harmed in the water but continue to watch, each week, as we reunite after our respective swims, their face resplendent. Merryn continues to survive. Each week they return from the ocean alive. My own anxiety, calmed somewhat.

Another Saturday, I drop Merryn off at the same spot, drive to Wylie's. I take my thermos and drink a coffee after my swim up on the deck overlooking the ocean. I curve my way back along the coast to the bookshop by the sea. 'Why don't you do your laps at Icebergs?' Merryn asks, with a hint of encouragement, seeing inside me a familiar battle between my need for routine and the perils of taking a risk. Icebergs is the sparkling ocean pool at Bondi Beach, a stone's throw from where swimmers disappear into the waves. It is picturesque, world famous. In my head it is the perfect pool, however I have never been. I have internalised every story about the people of Bondi, and a small part of me is afraid of how this freaky, hairy, trans body will be received there. It's untested and unknown. So, for weeks I dismiss Merryn's very sensible suggestion that may save me time and bring me a new, potentially positive experience.

The next week, I drive to Wylie's again, though the tide is high and the swell throws buckets of white wash over the edges of the pool and the sign across the pool's entry says the pool is closed.

For a brief moment I wish I had the courage to try the ocean.

For a few weeks, Merryn gently offers to come with me to Icebergs to 'try it out'. My anxious part gets in the way and I gently rebuff this kindness. I'm stuck on my story that the ocean is a risk too great to conquer and I cannot try something new. Change continues to petrify me, though underneath is a desire to be flexible, to push past it.

Merryn has found a community of ocean swimmers who plunge off the rocks at South Bondi into deep blue water way past the breakers. They swim together towards the pavilion and back. Bobbing around and looking out for each other. There is a Facebook group called Baby Swim and a kind, gentle water-wise ocean swimming aficionado called Meg, who swims Bondi's depths daily, is group mentor, offering her time and generous, calm expertise to a crew of people interested in the awe and wonder of the sea. Around her neck hangs a GoPro underwater camera. After each swim, when I pick up Merryn in the car, they will pull out their phone and show me Meg's pictures and tell me how brilliant it is to be under the ocean.

Over New Year's, some friends from Melbourne came to stay with us in our tiny worker's cottage. They brought with them their well-behaved deaf cattle dog, Ghost, whom our Remy loved instantly. Ghost is an old girl and Remy quickly learnt her place. I became proficient in thumbs up and a swift wave of the hand that signalled, 'Ghost, get out of the kitchen!' At dawn on New Year's Day, we drove to the rocks at South Bondi and watched the sunrise. There were people nearby, still munted from the night before yet surprisingly holding themselves together, taking in the splendour. They passed us and wished us a Happy New Year. Merryn pointed to the rocks where the baby swimmers dive into the sea. Afterwards we drove around the corner and parked at the beach. I sat in the car with the dogs as Merryn and our friends jumped into the water to welcome the New Year. I didn't bring my swimmers. Maybe on purpose. If I don't have them, I won't take a risk. I felt myself wanting to try. I said to Merryn that I wanted to get there someday, to be able to swim together. Merryn says that this is something they would love, and that each week at Baby Swim they say to the others, 'Each time we return, I keep hoping this will encourage Erin to come swim with us.'

On the first day of Year 8, I turned up to my high school to the news that today was only the first day for Year 7. I felt embarrassed but glad to leave. I called my friend Lisa from the blue payphone by the office and then caught the bus to the beach. We bobbed in the waves, went back to her place, ate pizza and played Nintendo 64. At thirteen I was not afraid of the ocean.

On a belting hot early summer Sunday I finally agree to go to Icebergs with Merryn. I push through my worry that there will be legions of lap swimmers and no space to find calm in the water. The enormous tiered concrete steps are blindingly white and filled with baking bodies. The pool's like any other, my worries unfounded, couched in myth and stories I've long told myself. It's busy but the 25-metre pool that sits perpendicular to the 50-metre showstopper is empty. I jump in, plough up and down. After a while I test out the larger pool and I do four quick laps, get back into the baby pool. I see Merryn. 'I can come here when you swim,' I say. 'I know,' they reply, smiling.

On the 30th July 2014, a one-metre, 30-kilogram Port Jackson shark found itself trapped in Wylie's Baths, having been washed in during high tide. I watched the video on the internet: a lifeguard and a photographer manoeuvre the chunky, distressed creature over the pool's edge with a towel, and one on each side, as if carrying an icebox, they deliver it back to the sea.

Inching towards risk, I drive with Merryn to Bondi early one morning over the Christmas holidays and we go in between the flags. The swell is mild and we are buffeted by waves. The water is clear and I am less afraid. Merryn emerges from underneath a spilling wave, 'I've got a present for you.' I am anticipating some seaweed in my face, but instead, they hand me a pair of goggles rescued from the seabed. It is my gift from the ocean and a sign to keep going.

The following week, Merryn's booked in for another ocean confidence course. They decided to go with their dad weeks before because I could not imagine going along. Sharks! Though I have been on a few ocean dips (no big swims), I'm sort of open to the idea. There are no extra spots but Merryn emails to request that if one comes up, to let us know. I wake to an email advising I can join the group. We turn up at Bondi for a three-hour crash course. We duck dive, learn to read the swell, decipher the surf report, locate a rip. We 'Superman' under breaking waves, ensuring more aerodynamism as we swim past the breakers. We learn to swim in a straight line and not get water in our mouths. We're far out past the surfers and wear bright yellow swim caps that read OceanFit. We bodysurf back to shore, where I'm amazed to see the instructor's trucker cap has stayed on all this time, even as he dipped and dived, effortless and smooth as a seal.

Merryn has a pair of swimmers that are mauve with cartoon bananas all over them. Some of the bananas are half peeled. I usually wear black speedos but I'm drawn to the bananas. There is a banana at the crotch and it gives the impression of an enormous cock.

Inspired by the memory of my three wet and blessed New Year's Day companions, I go with Merryn to Bondi again to try the waves for myself. 'Can I wear the bananas?' I ask. I have a surprisingly nice time under the water with the goggles the beach gave me.

The next day, we do it again. Only this time we swim out past the breaking waves, turn to continue parallel to the beach. We do quarter laps of the beach and back.

Because my breasts have shrivelled and shrunken into my chest like grapes left in the bottom of the fridge because of the hormones I keep in my sock drawer and rub into my arm each night before bed, the bananas are a little loose fitting at the back. I get Merryn to tie the straps together with an old highlighter-yellow shoelace, like a present. For some reason, I feel really faggy in this femme swim outfit – and am more comfortable in my gender and body than I can remember in a long time. Perhaps it is because it is so jarring: on exiting the water I return to the sand with pubes down to my mid-thigh, glued to my skin by the salt water. Pubes featuring that perfectly placed banana. The more my body is less readable as a woman's, the more it transgresses and resists the rules placed on bodies socially in gendered and binary ways, the more at home I seem to feel in outfits that before I leant into a medical transition, felt like another way for me to render myself invisible. I mean, it's the beach, no one really cares, and I, too, have less fucks to give. Regardless, the feeling is kind of profound, even if it speaks to this idea, one I am trying to free myself from, that strangers' understanding of my gender is important for it to be real. It isn't and I think this is one of the lessons the ocean is teaching me.

I like the bananas so much that I'm inspired by Bondi locals to seek out my own colourful pair that do not need continued strap-maintenance. I get myself a pair of Smugglettes, the women's version of Budgy Smugglers. As if women may not also wish to smuggle their budgies in them. They are pink with cockatoos all over them. They have thin straps and the thickness of my top half stands out and the grapes fit easily. The tag has a blurb that is both the worst copy and is so frighteningly gendered that I feel my brain bleed:

> Smugglettes are the Smugglers for chicks. All chicks! Those who love to kick a footy as well as even out their tan; chicks who can skull a beer as smoothly as they can braid each other's hair.

I turn up to Baby Swim. I swim to the pavilion and back under the tutelage of Meg. I am the first one back to the rocks – my final 200 metres spurred on by my momentary fear of death. I am ecstatic.

On a sunny Sunday, Merryn and I glide gingerly off the mossy shelf near Ben Buckler and swim the entire length of the beach. We stop momentarily, bobbing in the water. It is clear and my fear is mostly gone. We aim for Icebergs, get within 100 metres and turn back. We zigzag, behind and between surfers, next to each other and, using the pine tree as our sight guide, we heave ourselves back up onto the rocks with the help of the swell.

Merryn, perhaps strategically, bought a book exploring the concept of risk, *Into the Rip* by American journalist Damien Cave, at the centre of which is the story of moving his young family to Sydney and their experience of Surf Life Saving. I immediately connected with his anxiety about swimming in the surf, trying new things, his concern for his kids' safety at their local beach and navigating its famous rip, the Bronte Express. I felt the same things, though, as I was reading the book: I was moving towards exposing myself to the risks and anxieties I had up to this point allowed to be my story. Cave was experiencing a shift in how he felt in the world to which I could relate. I could see it in Merryn, too. Mastering a fear of the ocean, experiencing a sense of awe and wonder, was inspiring. Cave interviews psychologist Angela Duckworth, the author of *Grit*, about exposure therapy and its usefulness in pushing people past fear. She describes what I had been feeling every time Merryn returned from Baby Swim and each time I experienced my own ocean survival:

> Do hard things, realise that you don't die, that you or the other person is fine, and then it basically extinguishes your response.[13]

Clovelly Beach is a tiny strip of sand enclosed by concrete walls on either side and protected by a natural rock shelf that prevents the swell getting too dangerous. It's choppy sometimes and the water spills over the concrete ledges where on sunny days bathers sprawl on towels to picnic sans sand. At the far edge of the 300-metre inlet, closest to where it meets the ocean, the water is clearest near the rock wall and there are fish of all kinds darting around. It's deep and blue and there is a resident blue groper who meanders around looking surly if you swim too close. To enter the open ocean requires swimming out past the rocks. Merryn and I do laps up and down the skinny beach. We push ourselves into the swell and out past the rock wall, each time extending further into the ocean. 'Ten more metres that way,' I say, pointing towards the horizon.

Childhood, Cave notes in his book about risk, quoting a conversation with Duckworth, 'is actually doing progressively harder things and then extinguishing that natural fear response'.[14] For Duckworth, pushing past hard things is 'the foundation of all courage'.[15] Cave questions why as adults we often hold onto such fixed ideas of who we are or what we are capable of:

> Maybe that's the mistake we make in growing up as individuals and as nations – thinking of ourselves as 'grown', as completed and done learning. We stop exposing ourselves to risk because we think we no longer need courage. Instead of adding to who we are, we become museum pieces.[16]

It's funny to think of all I had missed out on because I thought this was me, done and grown. My story about the ocean was one that just 'was'. I'd never really interrogated it, for it was the only story I had; I couldn't imagine another one.

On a wild, wet Wednesday morning, I check the surf cam for Clovelly Beach. It's choppy. No one is in the water. I drive there and enter the water at the beach end. The swell makes it too hard to go all the way to the rock wall so I do half laps of the inlet. The water's murky and I end with twenty laps of the small ocean pool that is safely carved into the concrete shelf. Waves spill over the edge here too and it's hard going. I collect my bag from under the stairs and walk back to the car in rain that is getting heavier. There's only one guy in the water now, battling the froth in an attempt to get out. I look up to the lifesaver perched high in a protected box of tinted glass and wave a thank you.

I receive a text from Merryn while walking the dog, saying that a group of swimmers is going to enter the Cole Classic at Manly Beach the following weekend. A year later, I will come to know these swimmers, a crew of queer waterwise delights collectively known as the SUCKERS (Strange Underwater Creatures Keeping Everything Really Sexy) and I will join them on swims around headlands and islands and feel less afraid each time. We will have bright orange swimsuits made that we wear with such pride. The SUCKERS will advise on wetsuit quality and performance in the Facebook thread. We buy two, highlighter yellow and orange, and with the help of a trusty plastic bag, we slip ourselves into them on regular weekday mornings before sunrise when it's not raining and the swell is swell. Merryn's thinking of entering and asks if I want to go, too. My body stiffens at the idea of a big event, a swim with many other people – a race that's also not a race. Am I ready for it? How can it be fun? Can I push past my fear and extinguish it? It's the fortieth anniversary of the event, one that happens every February and fundraises for the Surf Life Saving Club. It's billed as a community event and there are one-, two- and five-kilometre swims people can enter. Merryn tells me that there is a 'back of the pack' swim you can do – which is for those who don't take it seriously and just want to have fun. I soften at this news – the idea of being at the back of the pack with Merryn and our friends from the SUCKERS leaves me open to it. I am invited into the Facebook chat of the SUCKERS and words of encouragement spill out of the screen: 'You can do it! We'll be at the back of the pack too,' says one; 'I'm bringing my fins so I can keep up,' says another.

I reply to these encouraging strangers and commit to back of the pack. I also imagine that this might be the safest way to swim a kilometre in the open ocean, with event marshals paddling about, ensuring everyone swims in the right direction. I briefly consider chasing back of the pack competitions around town.

We register for the back of the pack and a couple of days later we drive to Manly. In the Cole Classic there is no space for anyone outside the gender binary. You have two options only and so I am registered as a gender that I am not and I am wearing my cockatoos. We pick up our race packs from the registration table, a calico backpack, inside it a blue Cole Classic swimming cap signifying us as one-kilometre swimmers plus an electronic ankle monitor that will record our time. Merryn's friend Rita from work meets us at Shelly Beach and is our vocal cheer squad of one. She sees my golden hooped earrings and frowns: 'You'll get dragged back to shore in those!' She offers to mind them in a small metal container in which she keeps her crochet knick-knacks. We cannot find the other SUCKERS and so together we jump into the line of waiting back-of-the-packers in blue caps that is let out into the waves of Shelly Beach in batches of five or so swimmers every fifteen seconds. Owing to the conditions, we start and end on Shelly Beach, instead of the usual route which ventures further into Manly. We swim out 400 metres and take a sharp right turn at the first yellow buoy, swim to the next one, then head back in towards the beach where we exit the water and run through a blow-up finishing archway to the encouraging applause of strangers. The swim is easy, I glide in between other swimmers and feel present and alive. I swim over other people's feet and manoeuvre past slower participants. I put some of my ocean confidence course into practice and look up instead of to the side. I hardly swallow anything. It's choppy and when I look up, sometimes I see nothing but the top of the swell and where it hits the sky. I do it again, find the blue caps, follow them. The water is clear and I see hundreds of fish as I get closer to the shore. I push hard as we head back into the beach and swim quickly around a few stragglers who have stopped to convene their group. I run to the finish line. Rita is there, taking photos and screaming encouragement. I pull off my sandy, Velcro-ed ankle monitor and place it in a bucket held out for me by a kind volunteer. Rita and I stand by the finish line to wait for Merryn whom we cheer on as they emerge, smiling, from the ocean and run to the finish line. The SUCKERS are still swimming. We re-group then cheer the SUCKERS as they emerge from the ocean, one by one, out of breath and delighted.

Patrick

In his white hospital gown caked with remnants of his hospital lunch, his beard wild, yellowing at the mouth – it too, caked with food – Patrick earnestly told me he was lucky to be alive. For over six weeks I had been, without much luck, trying to get Patrick into supported aged care accommodation. Never a truer word had been said, I thought, feeling a cornucopia of emotions: a mixture of the usual frustrations of community work with a kind of deep, joyful affection for Patrick, whom I had simply, with creativity and patience, been trying to keep alive. In his clean(ish) gown, I felt a fondness for this jovial, ruddy faced man with a dementia who resembled a dishevelled Kris Kringle.

I sat next to him on the hospital bed as we leafed through photos in the booklet advertising the aged care facility where they had available a bed for him. He told me how incredibly 'modern' it looked and that he couldn't wait to move in. He said he didn't know what he would have done without me.

People say these kinds of things to community workers often, grateful that someone is on their side in the war against a welfare system that feels soul-crushing. Sometimes, they hate you, just another social worker there to interfere, to try and normalise life, to reduce risk and clip their wings. Sometimes, these relationships are one of few meaningful connections they might have, being so isolated from the world, alone in a place where accessing a basic quality of life or enjoying a sense of safety feels far beyond reach.

They're usually hyperbolic, these sentiments. They wouldn't have died without you, because they have lived a lifetime of pushing back against poverty and trauma and racism and abuse and unjust systems. They have been in and out of hospital and institutions and they have survived. It's a way of saying 'You're important to me, I can see how you might be trying to help me out'. That you being with them in the swamp is meaningful, even if the system remains the same. The Patricks of this world can see that you might be doing your best and that you see them for who they are, not how prevailing narratives construct them – as drunks, as homeless, as junkies, as outcasts, as unhinged.

Patrick's statement was no hyperbole and I couldn't help but smile at this, the outcome of his story.

Before I got into social work, I fucked about being anxious. I did an arts degree, took women's studies and found my family of queers, anarchists, punks and misfits. Activist queers. I learnt about community organising, mutual aid, prison abolition, the role of trans and queer liberation in the dismantling of other oppressive structures. I learnt that to be truly feminist, then we also must be actively working on being anti-racist and undoing deeply entrenched transphobia and whorephobia. I spent hours unlearning colonising beliefs, attending punk fundraiser shows for friends' gender affirmation surgeries (not covered by Medicare), dumpster-diving in the depths of the night, getting involved in movements that intersected with my own. I went to protests and babbled angrily into the internet. I read about the role of neoliberal capitalism in constructing and maintaining inequality in its endless pursuit of profit. I briefly joined a socialist group and when I told them I was going to be a social worker, they admonished me for being a reformist – not radical enough, they said. I cried my eyes out, and on my walk home, bumped into a friend of a friend, himself a social worker who held me in a soft and welcoming bear hug. I never went back.

Regardless of the acrid delivery of my comrades, there's something valid in that interpretation and it was one I shared. Social work's origins are complicated and reformist. Social work is a profession evolved from the early days of charity and religious benevolence. Though this system shifted over time, and indeed, social work has a much more progressive and anti-oppressive orientation now, there are still pervasive and individualist narratives around the deserving and underserving that continue to shape how society at large thinks about and works alongside the vulnerable and marginalised. Social work has often functioned as a technology of social control, even at its most reflective, and in working with those who do not fit into mainstream society, the role of caseworkers (often because there is such a lack of resources) has been about assisting those who are unable to function within the narrow confines of capitalist productivity better navigate its oppressive terrain.

When my community aged care casework team received the referral to go and visit Patrick, it was after he had fallen over while drunk outside his local Woolworths and hit his head. He landed in hospital, was kept overnight for observation and sent home the next day. I went sleuthing through his old notes. He had been in and out of hospital more than twenty times in the previous four years. He had not one support in the community.

His notes made sobering reading: Patrick is 'severely cognitively impaired'.

Another note: 'Non-compliant and cantankerous.'

Another: 'Discharged against medical advice.'

Another: 'Patrick was found wandering by ward staff upstairs naked and delirious, asking for directions to the bus station. He was assisted back to bed.'

I found a hospital discharge summary floating on his loungeroom floor, slick with greasy tuna brine.

Patrick lived a twenty-five-minute drive from my office in a house so squalid and cluttered that it was at times difficult to breathe.

He was an alcoholic ex-truckdriver who claimed to have once been Sydney's amateur arm-wrestling champion. He had lived in this house his entire life – it had belonged to his parents, who died, leaving it to him. He had no siblings, no living family, no connections. A broken shopping trolley was the centrepiece of his home. He slept on a pile of clothes and dirty linen strewn across a mattress on his bedroom floor visible through a window that overlooked a flourishing apricot tree which stuck out among a backyard long since mowed. When I met him for the first time, not long after he returned from hospital after his Woollies fall, he opened the door in a bright green skivvy, disintegrating Crocs on the wrong feet. He let me in, apologising for the state of things. He was, he said, in the midst of a renovation. His home resembled a rubbish tip and smelt of the sea. I visited every few days to make sure he was still alive. Each time his skivvy, a darker shade of green, encrusted with food and vomit and blood.

In 2015, the year before I met Patrick, the Commonwealth's Aged Care reforms decimated the kind of work being done in the community for people like him, crack-fallers who needed actual co-ordinated support to access services that might keep them alive because they lacked the capacity to set up services themselves. The banishment of specialised case management services sat within a far-reaching wave of neoliberal policy reform in Australia and is symptomatic of the shirking of state responsibility in a market-oriented system, one defined, more and more, by deregulation and privatisation. Services across the country for people over sixty-five that had existed since the mid-1980s have been mostly defunded or subsumed into aged care packages which require a degree of health literacy just to access.

What was once provided by the state in the form of social services shifted to the private sphere, with individuals needing to enter into private contracts with service providers. Healthcare was no longer a right but a product to be bought, provided you had the means. Like what's been witnessed in the United States, this kind of system created new categories of disenfranchisement, with people like Patrick virtually locked out of healthcare, unable to afford it or without the supports to access it.

One time Patrick opened the door and two black eyes stared back at me. His shirt was grubbier than usual and there was more detritus in his impressive beard than I'd ever seen. He let out an exasperated sigh on seeing me; he was expecting someone else.

With a focus on self-reliance and responsibility, neoliberal policy reform fails to make room for the significant barriers to accessing services, advocacy and supports faced by those with disabilities who simply cannot go it alone. Before they were wound down, case management services often functioned as the proxy for society's most vulnerable; the preventative supports designed to assist and advocate for those who couldn't do it themselves. Casework support, usually provided by social workers (who, in keeping with the neoliberal discourse, continue to be professionally erased and streamlined – genericised to 'care workers', 'linkers', 'carers'), was the mechanism that existed to comprehensively sustain, often over long periods, those most disproportionately affected by the onus on 'self-reliance' to actually access the privatised programs supposedly there to help them. It is messy, creative advocacy work. It involves words and tone and waiting on the phone and filling in forms and re-homing litters of kittens and filling up fridges at 5 pm on a Friday night. It is work with worth that cannot be captured by a key performance indicator. It is work that is at once immeasurable and invaluable. At times, it is invisible work, too.

Another three weeks later, I drive to Patrick's, as I always do, to check he is alive. I take him a sausage and egg McMuffin because last time he had the shits with me and told me to fuck off. I'm working on the guardianship paperwork, because without the proof that Patrick has a significant impairment that impacts his survival, I cannot ensure his safety or organise any housing against his will, which is what I must do now because none of my less oppressive creative efforts are working. This looks like suggesting some respite for while he does his renovations. 'Too busy with my jobs,' he tells me.

Community work can be slow and plodding. I told Patrick I'd be bringing my doctor friend around the next week. My colleague Margaret, a geriatrician in her late fifties, would rock up to joint visits in an ancient Morris Minor in her usual uniform of beige linen pants and a button-up long-sleeved shirt, her neck decorated with a colourful mass of clanking wooden beads.

She spoke with the gentleness of a therapist, open and curious and full of warmth. She had the capacity for instant connection and a clinical acumen that comes from years of assessing people in their own homes with dignity and care.

When we arrived at Patrick's, he wasn't home. We sat together outside his house, on the brick wall, out the front of his overgrown hedge, his front lawn littered with garbage and wet, semi-decomposed cardboard boxes. He emerged from around the corner, steadying himself with his four-wheeled walker. Patrick let go of the walker's handle to wave hello and immediately toppled over. I watched him, as if in slow motion, somehow gracefully bounce straight back onto his feet. Uninjured, he ushered us inside.

Rather than run though a set of questions to assess the person's orientation, insight and judgement, Margaret simply wove her professional queries into conversation. Pretending her watch was broken, she shoved it in front of Patrick and asked if he could help her read the time on the analogue clock-face. She asked him what month it was.

'It's October.'

It was January.

'How old are you?' she asked him next and he told us that he had just turned thirty-five.

She took out her wallet and into Patrick's hands placed a fifty- and a twenty-dollar note and one fifty-cent coin. She asked his help in counting how much money she had. One hundred and seventy bucks, he said.

He gave Margaret a tour of his house and told her about his renovations. There was a door dangling off one hinge like a loose tooth. The kitchen sink was full of dead flies. A soggy pair of once-white Y-fronts straddled the top of his television. There were five small bar fridges stacked in a corner but not one scrap of food in the house. An ancient bookshelf, rotting into itself and overloaded with dusty books and old arm-wrestling trophies, took up most of his front room.

The move towards privatising previously public services has meant the often chaotic and creative world of social work and community-based advocacy have been increasingly needing to prove, via quantifiable concrete data, a measurement of its worth and efficiency in the new market of risk-management.

Connected to this shift is an infusion of market values into social work settings (termed 'managerialism' or 'marketisation') whereby workers must prove their worth by demonstrating productivity and economic efficiency rather than by the ways they build relationships with individuals and communities and promote social justice. Grounded in the increasingly global principles of risk management, social work practice has become tightly regulated and standardised, not in order to advance social fairness but to ensure cost saving.

Canadian social justice activist and therapist Vikki Reynolds writes a lot about the work of community workers in the neoliberal era of risk management, productivity, KPIs and measurement. She posits that it is hard to measure the immeasurable. How to go about measuring the dignifying of people, the remembering of a name, the purposeful use of language that doesn't maintain stigma, gendering someone in ways that are affirming? How can we measure something that does *not* happen because community workers are around – the hospital admission prevented, the suicide thwarted? For Reynolds:

> The ineffable, intangible and untraceable influence of our collective work cannot be measured. Much of the work we do in the margins goes unmeasured for lack of an instrument of measurement, or because what we do achieve is not prioritised, or recognised as having value. I work to track and name immeasurable outcomes, so that our work is not disappeared. In particular I attend to dignifying clients, fostering safety, and unhappenings – situations that do not get measurably worse because of our work.[17]

The same problems anticipated in the lead-up to the 2015 changes, which were that costing out case management supports fails to acknowledge its critical value in the lives of our most marginalised elderly people, were the problems we saw play out in the community. In a system that privileges numbers and statistics and measuring success, community work is a place of mess and chaos and where the immeasurable outcome, the unhappenings, is where true 'success' lies. The awful irony, in looking back at the decimation of these services, is that their usefulness was finally seen only once they were disappeared, and things, awful things, started to actually happen. Life got worse for people. People were unable to access services due to impairment, older people died at home or experienced elder abuse without the input of previously funded specialised teams of aged care clinicians, people entered nursing homes or hospitals prematurely or under duress.

For someone like Patrick, whose severe dementia curtailed his insight and capacity to co-ordinate his own life, self-reliance wasn't something he could rely on anymore. Neoliberal policies in aged care in Australia – such as a move to consumer-directed care models and the obliteration of case management services – essentially cut out the 'in between'. The case management services, like the one I was a part of, is work now being done on the margins but in ways far less resourced than previously. It is recast under different names such as 'short-term support services' or 'older persons rapid response teams', and funded by state-based health services to fill in a gaping hole because we can see the system is broken.

The assumption is that people – whoever they are – can figure things out. And if they can't, then too bad. What this looks like in reality is that in a case like Patrick's, the support worker and service that might fill the gap – the gap between Patrick living in his squalid home, unable to advocate for himself and Patrick accessing services that meet his health-care needs and afford him some dignity – no longer exist in any substantial iteration. The cruel irony of accessing case management services is that without the capacity or means to do this on his own, he actually needs case management and advocacy to set up the supports in the first place.

After many weeks of trying to convince Patrick of the benefits of a clean and safe place to live, I couldn't get him into it. I challenged him to an arm-wrestling match – suggesting that if I beat him, he would have to at least indulge me and come and look at this aged care place I'd found. He said he'd retired long ago and wasn't coming out of retirement for that. Resigned to co-ordinating a public guardian for him instead, to help him make end-of-life decisions given the severity of his dementia, I pulled a report together. It was like a wild fairy tale that I wanted to ensure did not have a grisly ending.

The last day I visit him at home it's a filthy thirty-five degrees. I arrive at the front door and hear him crying out in pain. I find him splayed out, near naked on the floor, his pasty, emaciated chest covered in grit and sweat and sparse silver hair. His stubby shorts remain back to front, puffy at the groin. He'd tripped over the edge of a rug and couldn't get himself up. I call the ambulance and find a spot next to Patrick on the floor. I hold his hand while we wait.

And it is after all this that I find myself perched on the hospital bed, Patrick in his gown, his grotty beard full of lunch. I feel a sense of relief. He smiles in recognition when I wander in, his bossy visitor. He tells me about the nurse who had shown him some pictures of 'this new place' – the bathroom he tells me, is 'a little dated but still, quite alright'. It is the facility I had been encouraging we go and check out, that had saved a room for him for this hopeful conclusion. The gall! Patrick's own bathroom a miasma of shit and piss and blood and vomit.

'A little dated, huh?' I say, adjusting to the new reality, that I might not find him dead inside his squalid palace. He smiles, holds my hand, looks me right in the eyes. 'I'd be dead without you.'

Maggie and Olivia or: Flickering in and out of Many Things

In an interview filmed in 2016 at the London Review Bookshop, the non-binary author Olivia Laing is in conversation with author Maggie Nelson about her book, *The Argonauts*. Their immense brains are striking and conversation flows. At the beginning of the interview, Maggie takes a moment before reading a passage from her book to highlight her admiration for Olivia's writing, their 'overlapping points of kinship'.[18]

It's true, they have many threads of overlap. Especially how they write about gender, power, freedom and how bodies can be. I read *The Argonauts* when it came out, and again more recently, after Olivia's book *Funny Weather: Art in an Emergency* inspired a reread. Both writers have this beautiful capacity to weave together stories of the everyday while questioning the world and its structures – how people and systems and words (and the context in which these are spoken and understood) can be stifling, liberating or a combination.

Nelson and Laing's work reckons with power, queerness, the body, art, capitalism and the limits of language, especially when it comes to speaking about gender and its possibilities. Both are interested in opening imaginations to the fullness of humanity.

I was experiencing a sort of deep kinship with Maggie and Olivia and disappeared into YouTube and podcast wormholes devouring whatever I could find. I dived first into Maggie's 2021 interview with Olivia on the release of her newest book, *Everybody: A book about Freedom*.[19] After reading Olivia's *The Lonely City* a few years ago, I was obsessed with everything she had ever written.

Olivia's writing is the kind that stops the world, bold and wandering, curious and spacious. Words that weave ideas together effortlessly and inspire you to borrow more books, read more. Words that introduce you to new people and open up worlds. Her work is a nervous-system experience for me, its reading, simultaneously intellectual and bodily. It is hard to capture this kind of pleasure in words. For me it is akin to how a dip in the ocean brings more glimmer to a day, the way a fleecy jumper sits on the skin afterwards. A micro moment of tiny pleasure.

In the 2021 interview, Maggie thanks Olivia for hosting one of her favourite interviews of 2016. I quickly traced the links back in time to the bookshop in London and a role reversal. The duo is nestled behind what looks to be the front sales desk, as if working on an audit late into the night. The desktop computer almost obscures Maggie's face. A collection of multi-coloured Moleskin notebooks line the wall behind

Olivia's head. Olivia's hair has a soft and voluminous quality to it – loosely tied up high, light and airy, full of ideas.

Towards the end, Olivia references a press interview Maggie had done for *The Argonauts*, in which the journalist was annoyed that Maggie hadn't been more specific about her partner Harry's transition; 'wanting a concrete paragraph explaining who Harry was / is / became'. Olivia uses this example as a microcosm of society's obsession with categorisation, especially as it relates to gender, as if gender has become (or has always to a degree been) as Maggie deftly notes, the 'ultimate category of "what it is"'.

Olivia views *The Argonauts* as a book that captures the spirit of 'reparative reading' as described by queer theorist Eve Kosofsky Sedgwick in her essay 'Paranoid Reading and Reparative Reading; or, You're So Paranoid You Probably Think This Essay is About You'.[20] Both authors agree they still don't quite fully understand what Sedgwick is getting at in this piece – its academic thickness near impenetrable. The gist of it essentially being about how we approach meaning-making, how we understand the world around us.

Olivia suggests that the journalist's grasping for certainty is defensive, concerned with information gathering, identity, categorisation and the need to 'know'.

It struck me the interviewer's desire to have that clarified, to have a sort of before and after notion of what somebody's gender transition is – is a paranoid reading – and it's a paranoid reading that we're culturally obsessed with right now – the ... bathroom bills, the stuff about if somebody is

biologically female, this sort of horrific language that seems
very invested in finding out the truth of what a person is
. . . as if genitalia will tell you.[21]

Olivia talks of long being obsessed by Sedgwick's essay, at
what the academic's trying to get at. For Olivia, the concept
of reparative reading is 'to be fundamentally more invested
in finding nourishment than identifying poison. This doesn't
mean being naive or undeceived, unaware of crisis or undam-
aged by oppression. What it does mean is being driven to
find or invent something new and sustaining out of inimical
environments.'[22]

I loved Olivia's obsession with queer culture, especially
that of gay men, such as her delight in the work and life of
artist and activist David Wojnarowicz, whose biography, *Fire
in the Belly*, I'd read twice, years ago.

I have long held a rich fascination with gay men, and
Olivia's penchant for this topic of central importance to my
own identity was wild to encounter. Someone with the name
Olivia was writing about her obsession with faggots. I have
always felt like a faggot, a queer man who is not a man, but
sits close-to, in a body that is read as not quite. Many things
and none at all. To the world, I looked like an androgynous
woman and my fagginess was a mostly internal experience.
It sat mostly invisible to the world, understood by queers on
the fringes. An identity indulged and affirmed via the porn
I consumed, the art I liked, the sex I enjoyed, in the language
of lovers. I realise, to a degree, there is a pain in invisibility
but also in a paranoid reading – both my own and that of

the world external to me. A paranoid reading (one of course sitting inside a larger cultural capitalist hetero-patriarchal big P paranoia) of faggotry has not often had much space for the body that cannot be classified so neatly.

When I chanced upon, in Olivia's recent work, her definitive faggotry, I felt warm affinity:

> At the time, my own gender was like a noose around my neck. I was non-binary, even if I didn't yet know the word. I'd always felt like a boy inside, a femme gay boy, and the dissonance between how I experienced myself and how I was assumed to be was so painful that often I didn't want to leave my room and enter the world at all.[23]

At work, I received an email, one directed at my colleague and I. 'Hi Ladies,' it began. Out of all the possible collective nouns to choose from (this list to me seems endless), this one was a favourite among the people at work. I have also several times been addressed as 'girl' as in 'hey girl' but with that elongated 'urrr' sound in the middle – as if, subconsciously, they have a drive to just squeeze out the most discomfort from words that do not fit me. It is punishing, and yet my workmates hold no malice as they scrape burnt cheese off the sandwich press in the staff kitchen, smiling at my face full of moustache. 'Girl, how was your weekend?'

I look like Kurt Russell in *Escape from New York*. I wear button-up corduroy shirts, I dye my moustache and sometimes I wear earrings with a dangly silver chain. I do not look like a lady, in a binary sense, in the way I know they mean it.

I want for 'lady' to have little baggage – to be genderless and whatever one would like it to mean for them, but we do not live in that place at the moment. And so I viscerally crumple, another moment in which this body, its gender, is unrecognised, to a point of it literally vanishing in conversation.

There's this bit in *The Argonauts* which speaks so accurately of the dissonance of such cultural obliteration:

> Soon after we got together, we attended a dinner party at which a (presumably straight, or at least straight-married) woman who'd known Harry for some time turned to me and said, 'So, have you been with other women, before Harry?' I was taken aback. Undeterred, she went on: 'Straight ladies have always been hot for Harry.' Was Harry a woman? Was I a straight lady? What did past relationships I'd had with 'other women' have in common with this one? Why did I have to think about other 'straight ladies' who were hot for my Harry? [24]

I'd had my pronouns in the signature of my work email for a while, in the hope that including them might do the trick, maybe clear some of the semantic scrub out of the way. Nothing changed. The latest 'Ladies' left me so aggrieved I mustered the courage to try to shift this narrow and paranoid reading. I penned an email to all the people I ever had contact with at work with the subject line: 'I'm Trans / a request'.

I began my email with 'Hi Favourites' because these work people are both profoundly decent yet so deeply problematic, ensconced in what I like to think of now as a paranoid reading of everything. They are victims, too – of the limits of both language and the cultural obsession with categorisation, the needing to know.

Olivia Laing wrestles with this issue, too:

What I wanted as a trans person was to escape the binary altogether, which seems so natural if it includes you and so unnatural and violently enforced if it does not.[25]

For those who have not been lucky enough to have been born queer, these are not ways of living and thinking that come easily. In my workplace, I overhear women having conversations about babies. 'What is it?' someone asks the newly pregnant one, a question once posed to Maggie Nelson, to which she responded, confusingly, 'Ah . . . it's a human baby!?'

In my email I pointed out my gender, as well as the harm that can stem from not thinking about how heavily language is gendered. I assertively asked people to use my name or 'they' as a pronoun, sent out some resources and thanked them in advance for their efforts to affirm my gender at work.

Sedgwick's idea of reparative reading is also, maybe at its most simple – which is mostly all I can garner from it (which is absolutely enough!) – about the interplay of reading and language. It is not only about how we approach the world but also in how our approach influences how we choose to speak about it. A reparative reciprocity. A circular motion, in which curiosity about language leads to a curiosity of, and openness to, what it is attempting to make and create meaning of.

I like the idea of placing a reparative lens on the body and am curious what it might mean to come to bodies and gender from a less paranoid positioning. (I think of the paranoid position as a default cis-hetero-sexism with its stubborn drive to categorise people as man / woman.) If we come to people and the world with a more curious outlook, instead of giving in to the urge to classify, we create a space of openness where reparative work can be done.

Much like talk therapy, there is a lot of benefit in being able to accurately notice when we are dysregulated, because we can learn ways to respond that align with our values – to be less defensive and have compassion for the parts of us that have been primed to respond defensively. When we're in an activated state, triggered by our nervous system's hyper-speed responses to cues of danger, we haven't much capacity for curiosity, because our system gets too overloaded and our cognition diminishes. The paranoid positioning is akin to living in this constant fight or flight mode. We are quick and reactive, we are seeking safety from danger (the unknown) – and sometimes it feels unsafe if we cannot categorise, know and control.

There is something quite liberating in a reparative positioning, I think, especially as it relates to the body and to gender. It can impact how we see the world, who we see, what we see and how we understand ourselves. A curious approach to gender, a reparative approach, is one that challenges the crippling and oppressive edges of words and makes space for them to be refashioned anew.

Nelson, in the opening to *The Argonauts* writes that:

> Words change depending on who speaks them; there is no
> cure. The answer isn't to just introduce new words [. . .]
> One must also become alert to the multitude of possible
> uses, possible contexts, the wings with which each word
> can fly.[26]

I affirmed my gender long before I ever took hormones
to help bush-ify my moustache. Actually, that is not the
fullness of it because it was not really all my doing, I realise.
It was the reparative positioning of others that affirmed my
gender, too. It was in the words whispered into my ear by
lovers, 'Your dick is so hard.' Like when I call my partner my
boyfriend, when I say 'good boy' and when they say it back.
Language gave to me the body I knew was mine and brought
into existence so many possibilities for what my gender can
be. My partner's reparative positioning to my queer body
is less concerned with definition, certainty, binary – and
embraces the reality of surprise – thereby affirming me
from the inside out. The reparative reading of my body has
been, come to think of it, one of the greatest gifts of my
queer life.

Sedgwick in the erudite essay speaks to the idea that
because the reparative reader

> has room to realise that the future may be different from
> the present, it is also possible for her to entertain such
> profoundly painful, profoundly relieving, ethically crucial
> possibilities as that the past, in turn, could have happened
> differently from the way it actually did.[27]

She goes on to ask: 'Where does this argument leave projects of queer reading in particular? With the relative deemphasis of the question of "sexual difference" and sexual "sameness".'[28]

I take this to mean that reparative reading is a trans reading, one less concerned with binaries and definitions than it is with playing a role in the expansion of queer understandings and possibilities. Like Olivia, I had no language for the middle ground of gender in which I have always found comfort. Although holding a reparative positioning in this regard is exciting for a future in which binaries are less important and our gender is valid, I'm saddened that these reparative readings were not available to our younger selves, since their omission from cultural possibility and understanding impacted how lives were lived.

Carving out spaces for the likes of Olivia and I – faggots on the spectrum – has always been limiting, so insufficient. Sedgwick answers her own question:

I think it will leave us in a vastly better position to do justice to a wealth of characteristic, culturally central practices, many of which can well be called reparative, that emerge from queer experience but become invisible or illegible under a paranoid optic.[29]

Sitting on the couch recently, my partner asked me about what my aim might be, in terms of affirming my gender. We had not spoken much about it in a while – the changes are so slow and subtle day to day that it's mostly not a topic of conversation. They asked what I had in mind and if I had a goal of how I wanted to look and feel in my body. Whether if I went ahead with top surgery, did I think I might want to continue towards a more binary transition. Or if I still felt the same desire to find the middle space that has always been home to me.

I had started hormones to find a more ambiguous physicality, though remain on a full masculinising dose. What this means is that, if I do not reduce it, I will in a few years be read socially as a man. I am still misgendered in the world; at the shop, at the dog park, at the cafe, at work, at social gatherings, generally at most places. My answer to my partner's question was that my aim was not to be misgendered and that maybe I would continue the dose until fewer people called me 'lady'.

'That might never happen,' my partner said, reminding me of transmasculine friends, even those who had undergone a full binary transition, some even with flourishing beards, who still experienced being 'ma'amed' at the shops.

My outlook, I realise now, was a paranoid one, when I think of things in the way encouraged by Olivia and Maggie and Eve. Perhaps I have it all wrong, and may well have bastardised the latter's beautiful academic ideas. Even if I have (sorry, Eve), this idea of the reparative versus the paranoid has at least got me thinking. I have, for a long time, wanted the world to see me as I know myself to be – a queer faggot, not a woman, not a man. I appreciate this is a tough ask of a system that is completely paranoid and predicated on containing, naming and finding out the 'truth'. Gender is fluid, whereas paranoia is stuck in the mud.

It is not a stretch to think that queers might be susceptible to such readings, for we too are members of the paranoid external world, constantly battling against and within structures around us that contribute to the pains in the first place – namely patriarchy (with its attendant misogyny), power, language, gender norms and how these factors play out daily.

I wanted hormones to change me in ways that might mean some people would not be so quick to call me a lady, and also to feel more connected to my body. However, I did not want my faggoty middle ground to be rendered invisible, to be later mistaken for a man. Indeed, if the system is mostly paranoid, and forces us to live in black and white, my partner is right and my desire to be 'properly' read may never truly be achieved.

In reviewing *The Argonauts*, Olivia reminds us that Maggie is bent on using these kinds of experiences – in her case, partner Harry's constant experiences of being misgendered – to pry

> the culture open, of investigating what it is that's being so avidly defended and policed. Binaries, mostly: the overwhelming need, to which the left is no more immune than the right, for categories to remain pure and unpolluted [. . .] Individuals migrating from one gender to another, let alone refusing to commit to either, occasions immense turbulence in thought systems that depend upon orderly separation and partition.[30]

Maybe a reparative positioning of gender and the body is one in which curiosity about what a body can be both in language and in physicality is made possible. In maintaining some kind of transitional turbulence. Perhaps this is achievable by not making life easy for the paranoid system – which, in my case, I was trying to do when using its limited vocabulary to try and signal to it. There I was, waving madly across the dog park: see me as I am, as my boyfriend does when they turn to me in bed in the morning and say, 'Your moustache looks so beautiful today.'

I have held tight onto the idea that interactions with other people were a way to gauge my own gender expression, as if somehow it is not legitimate unless it is recognised by everyone. (That said, of course, we know ourselves through relating with others, and not being affirmed for a long time can be very painful.) As if, when someone at the dog park finally looks at me and umms and ahhs and fumbles over their words, and cannot box me in, then I'll know it's time to go get a new script, get off the full dose. This will signal that I'm finally 'here' at my destination. As opposed to, I fucking live here already and have always been here. A paranoid system is one in which people reach for the category that lives closest to what they know – it is the reality of a system that is not big enough for fringe dwellers, yet is nevertheless expanding. I realise, in trying to signal within its narrow remit, with its limited language, I deny others the opportunity for reparative reading, or to be a body among others, like Olivia's, that can be part of a reparative movement towards the body and to gender in this dreamy moment.

In *The Argonauts*, Maggie Nelson writes that before meeting Harry, she had spent a lifetime devoted to Wittgenstein's ideal that the inexpressible is contained – inexpressibly – in the expressed! This idea gets less airtime than his more reverential 'Whereof one cannot speak thereof one must be silent,' but it is, I think, the deeper idea. Its paradox is, quite literally, *why I write*, or how I feel able to keep writing.[31]

Perhaps a reparative positioning of the body and gender is that express-ability comes into being via people who, by somehow unburdening themselves of the paranoid lens (resisting the outside paranoid pressure of needing to help people 'know', which, for me, remains very difficult) bravely continue to exist in bodies and genders like Harry and Olivia and mine with the understanding that words are not yet good enough.

Towards the end of her interview with Olivia at the bookshop, Maggie speaks about her experiences of doing press for the book. Many times she had this sentence in her head, gifting it finally to Olivia:

It's not *The Crying Game*, okay . . . I'm like, do you get out much? . . . Because a lot of people live in a world where you might fuck somebody when you're not totally sure what their gender is – it happens, you know.

In some ways, the non-binary trans body is a reparative object (a hot one), and by just existing, it can pry open the space Olivia speaks about – to allow for Eve's dream of doing justice to this 'wealth of characteristic' that was simply invisible under the paranoid gaze.

Maggie reminds the audience at the bookshop of the good news that it's possible to be shifted from one optic to another and that one of the things that can get us there is 'being close to people who flicker in and out of many things'. There's something quite poetic in the idea of gender as a constant flickering, a shining in and out. Not static but constantly on the move, bright and luminescent. It feels full of possibilities, drained of paranoia. My new pronoun, at the bottom of the email, reads 'Them' – that one flickering in and out.

The Wedding

'How can you love yourself and be in a relationship with them?'

This was my friend Nate on the phone to me, a month after the wedding. In his cowboy best he'd read the poem 'Everything that was broken' by Mary Oliver during the ceremony. Strangely, the poem's content became a motif of sorts for the day that followed. Nate was my beloved's first ever love and one of the best friends I've ever made. His existence to us both individually and as a couple, central to our story.

He was talking about my parents, both of whom had behaved terribly at the wedding. He was also talking about the many things that had happened since, including the gaslighting email I had just forwarded him. My dad's response to an email I'd sent to my parents, whose deafening silence after the wedding had left me baffled. 'Precious, precious, precious' was the title of the Word document attached to his email – inside the body of which he had signed off 'your disappointed dad'.

Their behaviour was so shockingly bad that I was now left with decisions I never imagined I'd have to make. The rupture so painful I was reimagining my ongoing relationship with them. I'd been forced to reflect and reckon with the stories I'd long been telling myself, out of survival maybe, out of a history of minimising my own trauma, about my parents' capacity to show up for me, to love me, in the way I needed them to.

It is a strange feeling to hold both intense joy and grief in your hands at the same time. Sometimes they merge, like plasticine, into one colourful greasy ball. In others, they are separate and sit neatly side by side. I have not had a day that has filled me up so thoroughly nor have I experienced parental failure so profoundly as the day I vowed to Merryn that I would not deceive them unless I was planning a special surprise and that I would nourish our friendships as solidly as I would nourish our love.

The wedding had been postponed twice before we wed, mid-June under a tree in the Hunter Valley by our delightful friend Frankie who also happened to be a celebrant – a mere five steps away from a large shed in which our favourite hundred or so friends gathered to celebrate our love and dance on bright green Astroturf until 11 pm, before which we had formed a tunnel to farewell the eight people who had to leave early to catch the bus home. We planned to fuck things up at our wedding. Tradition, stories, how things were supposed to be done.

Merryn and I took the week off work before the wedding to get all the admin done. We picked up boxes of booze from the shop, shoved it in the car, Zoomed with the caterer, made best friends with Kal the wedding planner for the venue, who told us on the night that it was the best wedding she'd ever been to and even though it was her actual job she didn't want to go home. We put names into a primitive Excel spreadsheet ('the puzzle') that served as a seating plan, crunched the numbers, answered RSVP emails and paid bills. COVID meant many people pulled out and Merryn would sit for hours, knees curled beneath the laptop, completing, with ostensible glee, the puzzle. Once, when I asked them how the puzzle was going, they looked up at me, and told me earnestly how 'absolutely satisfying' it was.

You might imagine such a puzzle to be easy, but it is not. When you host a queer wedding, where so many lives are entwined, sometimes there are delicate relationships to navigate, long feuds to avoid. And, so, often we looked at the puzzle, shuffling names around – these eyes to this back, this person on the same side of a long table, far enough away to be able to hold their own.

I had fucked only one guest previously, though COVID prevented a few more. The American anarchist watched it online during a night shift between delivering babies. Our lives, wildly different now. Merryn's entire wedding party, mostly exes of some kind.

We were married in reds and crimsons and pinks. Merryn in a pink suit embroidered in reds and whites with pearls all over, like a regal, faggoty Elvis. A three-metre-long crimson veil streaming from the shoulders trailed behind them like a cape. I wore a blood-red velvet vest and high-waisted pants, underneath it my signature item, a $35 H&M long-sleeved laced high-necked top. On top, a pearl shoulder piece. Merryn's mum and grandmother's wedding day pearls sat atop a freshly done set of braids in which we also somehow managed to weave in a small white veil. Like a grown-up queer Little Lord Fauntleroy. Remy wore a pink and black tuxedo, which was really just a flashy bib attached to a collar. Our friend walked her out on the lead as one of our twelve best people who led us down the Astroturf-ed aisle from the enormous house we'd rented on the property, peeling away to either side of the spot we were soon to find ourselves, beneath the tree.

During the ceremony, we gave our rings out to the crowd, to be held and passed through the warm hands of those we love. My friend Bay later told us that she had made sure to rub both the rings on Remy before she handed them on. When Frankie mentioned the rings going out, I could hear Mum, who was sitting in the front row, give out an exasperated sigh, heckling, 'Ooh that'll take all day!' Frankie managed her well, but I remember feeling betrayed by Mum in that moment. That waiting for me to be wed was a thing to be endured.

For the ceremony, we had put our parents in the front row. I was mostly grinning at Merryn, at our friends' faces as we walked out hand in hand, all of them grinning back at us and hollering and hooting as if we were celebrities. This was our day and I could already feel its warmth. Mid-ceremony I felt a pain at the back of my head, from so much smiling. I could see my parents in my periphery, both seemingly half present: Dad, back curved and slouched forward, looking into his hands, barely looking up. Mum, similarly vacant, in a way that betrayed an absence.

During the speeches, where the most damage would be done, I watched on as Merryn gave their speech. Later when they would ask me what my favourite part of the day was, one of the moments I loved most was when they called me 'strange'. Dad looked straight ahead, never at Merryn as they spoke of our love story, about our idiosyncratic chaos being in perfect equilibrium.

Before the day, I often said to Merryn that I was looking forward to having Mum and Dad truly see our queer life. They would question me, remind me that some of how I showed up in the world still came with how I was approved of or validated by other people. Sure, Merryn said, we want them to experience it, but that is not the point of the wedding day. You are already important, whether they see this or not.

Merryn was right. I'd done a lot to shift this seeking of approval in my life, by nourishing and making space for my own inner life, for excavating patterns of the past. Patterns of being good, saying yes, people-pleasing in return for the love of my parents, later the love of others; staying small to stay emotionally safe. In my family system, I'd finally come to realise, staying small was evident in my never properly making space for the fact I was trans until I was thirty-six.

Even so, the urge to be seen and understood by my parents, in my authenticity, on which I had spent so long and so much work growing into, was still a thing for me. The urge to be seen, respected and understood is big in families. In the most formative and impactful attachment relationships we have, there is a biological drive to be seen and loved and respected for all that we are. When we don't get it in the way that we need, when we, as small kids, get a whiff of having to earn our parents' love – an inkling that it is conditional on certain types of behaviour, certain ways of being; when we have deciphered for some reason that our selfhood is not enough, that we are shameful, we are too this or too that – we adapt magnificently in surviving our young life. We banish the aspects of self that don't gain our parents' approval (the too gay parts, the too trans parts, the too this too that parts) because if they show up, we risk losing love altogether. We then take the internalised story that we are bad as we are, shameful, too this too that, not enough – and as adults we infect our entire life with lies born from our creative survival. I am getting better at unpicking the lies that have infected my life, partly thanks to the work I am trained to do. I see people in my work who have also lived with a heavy load of lies; some of them, for their own emotional safety, still buy into them.

I say to them, when you are eight years old, you cannot just pack up your small wheelie bag and take yourself to the Airbnb and start living your bold, authentic life. You have to keep your parent/s in a place of power and authority because you need to believe that to ensure your own safety. And so you internalise that your parents' anger, neglect, big enormous chaotic mood swings, their belittling of your queerness, your strangeness, your vulnerability is because you must be terrible.

When it was my time to speak I could feel my dad's not-looking. His face never landing on me. I could see his avoidant eyes. It was painful and I chose to look mostly at Merryn and, on occasion, swept my eyes over the room. He sat five metres from me, in my velvety finery. I felt so solidly myself and I knew, for reasons that sit outside of me but are hard to remember when your parent cannot seem to meet your eyes, that he could not bear to see me.

In the weeks leading up to the wedding, I asked Mum to use the pronouns I'd long been using in life. I emailed her some resources, which were couched in my usual thoughtful, overly responsible, emotionally manage-y style. I was anticipating Mum's distress, her taking of this request as critique as opposed to what it was: me asking, simply, for a need to be met.

This is a style familiar to that adult child who has played a certain role for too long. Be the family peacemaker, holder of secrets or surrogate counsellor. A role that extends from the development of a false self that was honed to receive love but is actually a rubbish role to continue long term for it maintains a system that never works for our authenticity – it remains hidden. We continue to mask it, out of habit. My habits, of managing Mum's emotions, were still present in our dynamic.

I had not, in the years before, asked much of my parents in the way of using new pronouns, mainly because it was something I had little capacity for and they were, in my mind at least, loving and curious enough. They are older boomers and it was a new concept, but I felt mostly accepted by them. This request, funnily, was not just for me but also for the freaks like me who'd be at the wedding, whose gender neutrality it would be important to honour.

I was walking Remy at Sydney Park when I called Mum – we were on the stepping stones in the pond in the belly of the park. Remy refuses to wee in a slightly damp backyard, preferring to give herself urinary retention, but will roll her whole chiselled body in a cesspit of mud in the blink of an eye. We have a strategic walk, one that always ends at the pond where I stand on the stones and throw treats into the water so she can wash. She won't put more than half her body in but at least her feet get clean.

I asked Mum about the email I had sent as I threw Remy her treats. Mum's voice quivered, my request for a pronoun adjustment, for her, adding to her own deeply held 'not good enough' story. I had offered to have friends help edit her speech for her, which she mistakenly took as editing the content, not the simple find and replace situation which I'd intended, but absolutely did not feel after the wedding, when she poured so many 'shes' into one wedding speech that, in another setting, she might have won some kind of linguistic honour. 'I've been edited my whole life,' she sobbed into the receiver. She had decided that not to give a speech – the ultimate act of not fucking it up – was the safest option. I spent the rest of the phone call in my familiar role, managing her emotions, making space for her big feelings. I made a slip of space for myself, reminding her that I was giving her the opportunity to try, that this would be a way of loving me. That she could fuck it up, as long as the intention was there. I called her bluff and said, if she didn't want to do it then that was up to her. I ended the call, exhausted.

A week later, I texted Mum. Yes, she and Dad would be speaking.

A few days before the wedding, Mum had contacted Frankie, the celebrant, wanting some advice about her speech, as she was having difficulty speaking about me in the

197

past. Without 'she', what *was* my past, how to speak about it? To her, it was as if asking for 'they' as a more liveable, comfortable gender label left me in a sort of 'before' and 'after' zone. That the past was off limits. To Mum, using 'they' for the past was beyond comprehension. For her, it was as if the past wouldn't be the same with the replacement terminology, could not be spoken of, unless in the way knowable to her: as 'she', my daughter. Thing is, there was no before and after, just a new, closer-to name for my gender, which has always been the same.

Frankie linked us into her reply to Mum and tears formed when I read Frankie tell Mum what a gift of vulnerability my opening up was, an opportunity to be let into my authenticity. That I had likely been:

> allowing other people to call them something that they don't like, that they in some ways endure, and have endured potentially for years, even if they had not yet come to a place to articulate it. Now they have articulated it, and given us the privilege of that insight.
>
> I think of all the years that people in this situation have endured being called something they are not, and in some cases really hate, because it keeps everyone else happy.
>
> So by adopting their preferred pronouns – not just for now, but in reference to who they are holistically, including the past, we (me included) are allowing Erin (and Merryn) to be able to be who they are, to be comfortable. Which feels like a great thing ordinarily, let alone on their wedding day.

It's a good sign, we thought, Mum asking for support. A few days later Frankie was reassured that Mum had 'got it'.

In the years before getting married, I'd taken myself back to therapy. I believed there was still some family of origin work to do, especially around my mum, with whom I was less entangled but felt tremendous guilt about. A friend recommended a book about the Mother Wound and it really rang true – it was a deep dive, and one that made me reckon with the ways in which my relationship, my patterns with Mum, had kept me small. I'd lent it to a friend who cannot bear to leave her small toddler alone with her own mother, who continues to demand to see the grandchild when it suits her needs, not my friend's. This friend, so mortified after the wedding, shoved the book back into my hand a few days later and encouraged me to 'read it again' for some solidifying insights, maybe some solace.

The Mother Wound, essentially, is the idea that patriarchy, in its systemic disenfranchisement and wounding of women (and again, this is a gendered theory but I think very much is about the experiences of people, but and especially female-socialised people in relation to their mothers) via sexism and gender norms, sets women up to perpetuate this wounding cycle unconsciously in their mothering by passing on damaging beliefs and behaviour to their daughters.

Bethany Webster, in *Discovering the Inner Mother*, talks about the Mother Wound as being something that happens on an individual level, on a cultural level as well as on a spiritual and planetary one. The personal Mother Wound is defined as:

a set of internalised limiting beliefs and patterns that origi-nates from the early dynamics with our mothers that cause problems in many areas of our adult lives, impacting how we see ourselves, one another, and our potential.[32]

Webster contextualises the Mother Wound historically; how it has become a culturally mandated position for most women, yet then also something oppressive given the unequal set-up of society, and at the same time something to which mothers are held to outrageous standards that leave them in a wild position of having to relinquish ambitions, serve everyone else's needs, stay hot and fuckable and skinny, manage a house, not complain and also probably go back to work and keep managing it all.

Essentially, society's unspoken messages create these limiting beliefs, and so:

women forgo their dreams, bottle up their desires, and suppress their needs in favour of meeting the cultural idea of what womanhood should be. The pressure is suffocating for most women, engendering rage, depression, anxiety, and overall emotional pain, which – when not addressed, as is often the case in patriarchal cultures – is then unconsciously passed on to daughters through subtle or even aggres-sive forms of emotional abandonment (mothers can't be emotionally present when stressed), manipulation (shame, guilt, and obligation), or rejection. Children interpret these moments of maternal abandonment, rejection, or manipula-tion as, 'There is something wrong with me,' 'I'm responsible for my mother's pain,' or 'I can make my mother happy if I'm a good girl.' This makes sense when one considers the limited cognitive development of a child, who sees herself as the cause of all things. Left unaddressed, these unconscious and untrue beliefs at the very core of the Mother Wound can negatively affect every area of our lives.[33]

Webster makes the point that the Mother Wound is a spectrum thing, with more supportive mother – child dynamics on one end and traumatic mother – child relationships on the other. Due to patriarchy's inherent misogyny, there's a cultural Mother Wound that impacts women individually in different ways:

> How she sees her own body, her potential, and her relation-ships. However, having a solid, healthy, loving relationship with our mother – one in which we are valued and cele-brated for our individual, separate selves while still deeply connected with our mother – protects or buffers us from some of the virulent impacts of cultural patriarchal beliefs about women.[34]

And so, this is how we come to know what is possible for our life. As children, we internalise, unconsciously, a certain set of limiting beliefs – and they 'have been deeply fused with our deepest human need for love, safety, and belonging'.[35]

Healing the Mother Wound is done on an individual level, at the level of being a child (I don't want to perpetu-ate the weird 'daughterliness' of the text – though I get what she means) of a mother. In understanding the ways in which we have internalised limiting beliefs via the dynamics we've experienced in our families, in decoupling the inherited beliefs from our need for safety and love, the better we are at striding into living a more authentic existence. It's not about blaming our mothers but about the systems in which they found themselves, their own systems of family entanglements – those too awash in patriarchy.

I started therapy over ten years ago when my Mother Wound was almost septic. Back then, I truly believed I was the cause of my parents' difficult marriage. I was a kid with ADHD and OCD, who was anxious, was having a very hard time being bullied at school and mucked up a lot. I yelled at my parents because I didn't cope very well with change. And so, I believed I needed to spend my adulthood making amends to them, being the 'good' kid. I was gay, too, and so I was probably also making up for that. I was especially trying to show up for Mum. I was her surrogate counsellor and we were in some ways quite emmeshed. Most weekends, I'd take her flowers and coffee and hear about the fractures of her marriage, her depression. I felt her sadness and her rage as my own and I was angry with my dad on her behalf for the ways I could see her belittled, not cared for. She would complain about my dad and my sister and do very little of her own inner work to shift or make a change.

Thankfully, she was not the kind of mother who placed the usual pressures on me (no demand for grandkids, say), and didn't ask too much about my personal life. Sometimes she would see me silhouetted in the doorframe when I arrived to visit, once with a new, very short haircut and ask why I had to make myself 'so unattractive'. When I started drawing on my moustache with eyeliner, before I actually grew one, Mum would have something to say about it, usually that I'd look nicer without it. These quips stood next to Mum texting me a photo of her at a rally, next to a queer anti-nuke campaign flag. 'I see you,' she was trying to say. She'd rescued Eddie Ayres's book from her own street library to give me. His transition being the key element of that book, which she had read, being a classical music fanatic and thus having listened to Eddie on the radio for years. Mum didn't request my overtures to her, gestures I felt duty-bound by. I gave them out willingly, born from our early years together and my ongoing belief that this is how I get seen.

Sometimes she'd cut out some queer stuff from the paper and slip it in a plastic sleeve because she knew I'd like to read it. Once she got so close, cutting out an article on a non-binary writer, who like me, was socialised female – 'Look at this bird!' she said, full of good intention. She remembered stuff like dates and special events. At times I felt so seen and understood, and at others, invisible. My transness was one of the things I felt I could not name to myself, let alone in front of her and it was not something I indulged as a possibility for years because of my fear of rupturing my family again. The idea that I was hurting them, disappointing them, was still clanging about inside.

Over time, I continued to do the work. I started to shift the ways I showed up without talking about it, I just refused to be that person anymore. I didn't think about it too deeply, rather just enacted a bit of a move away. I shifted the boundaries because I wanted to say yes less. I dipped in and out of my family like a backyard hot tub. Separate but close enough not to be hurt, to try and grow myself.

For a long while I didn't believe I was worth much and so when I had relationships, people could give me very little and it felt like the world. I had grown to value the part of me that showed up, that helped and rescued others – this was the way I honed myself in my family system. I valued this aspect of myself so much it influenced my career choice, though thankfully, now, I have learnt that it is not the only currency for validation I need to use anymore. Back then I had less belief in my intrinsic worth and found it more in how others saw me, and so I peppered my relationships with multiple acts of care and kindness and not asking for very much. I felt comfortable when managing other people's emotions, being available at the drop of a hat, stomping all over my own needs, which I found difficult to even name. I was like a crazed Hansel/Gretel combo rushing about doing backflips for people as I opened my mouth for some crumbs. I hurt so much but I was not aware of the patterns.

When I was dating the American, we took a trip to a Blue Mountains cabin. I went to the Blackheath Pool to swim laps. I came back and she had made a pot of coffee for us. I couldn't believe this act of kindness. I almost died. I told this story to my friends later on, gobsmacked by this outrageous display of love. 'Can you believe it?' I had said to them. 'She made me a pot of coffee!' I portrayed it as one of the most loving things anyone had ever done for me, and their eyes bulged in horror as one of them told me outright that this was the least I deserved.

My friend Vicki is a small Greek dyke who is the most generous, caring and wise person I know. She is an accidental comedian who commands the attention of any room she steps into. She is full of integrity and wit. Because she led a queer double life, the early years of our friendship happened at my flat and at our friend's Lebanese restaurant in Bankstown, where all our queer friends would gather and eat leftover felafel and fattoush and smoke joints late into the night. Vicki was single for many years, so solidly happy in her own life she told me that she only needed to be in a relationship when that person was right – her life was full already. She told me she was in need of nothing but the best. I treasure her advice, as it's always been spot-on. Her capacity to be so solidly in herself and on her own was inspiring to me. I wanted the capacity to reassure myself that I was enough, too. Vicki was the MC at the wedding and held the night together so beautifully for Merryn and me. She talked about how my life had been on turbo in the last four years – a sort of personal progression those close to me have really seen.

Just after Vicki had told people the story of the week prior, when Merryn and I had met her at a cafe for a wedding run-through where she had a runny nose and I pulled out a doggy bag from my pocket convinced I had the solution, she welcomed Mum to speak. Nestled at the outer edge of the seating plan, with ready access to the bar, I listened, watched. I was astonished as Mum delivered a speech so bewildering, so strange that my system shut down. What followed was a sort of life-recap in which she gave a comprehensive list of the most traumatic and intimate aspects of my childhood. My obsession with rewriting the dictionary (a literal offshoot of my debilitating OCD), how I was bullied at school, my aversion to stockings, dubious haircuts, the signs I was different. My perfectionism. Her own sort of detective-like thinking about how she knew I was gay because a boy came over and slept on a trundle bed. That time I got 99 per cent on a maths test and sobbed about the 1 per cent. How I was dux of my high school and then still flagellated myself because it was a 'sports high' and still wasn't good enough. She had cards in front of her, apparently on which this speech was written. She had somehow planned what felt and looked like someone confabulating. She misgendered me and used 'she' so many times that if it was a drinking game everyone would have died.

I felt the room die. The mood dropped and there was a heavy stillness. It was as if everybody had stopped breathing. Merryn and I looked at one another, their hand on my knee, eyes full of horror but also full of love and solidarity. 'What do you want to do?' I was frozen, shrunken in my chair. I was motioning to Mum from afar, hands across my body in a cross, signalling *Please, please stop*. Friends made eye contact from across the room, concerned eyes that asked if we were okay, eyes that held so much love and worry and care. *We see this too, we're witnessing this with you*, they offered silently. Most were looking down at the table in front of them. Even Gillian the photographer had stopped taking photographs and just stood there, motionless, camera dangling loosely by her side. I saw queer friends get up and leave the room.

Nate came over to us, crouched down behind our seats. 'Do you want me to cut her off?' he asked. With a hand on my shoulder, another friend offered to do the same. 'What do you want us to do? If you want this to stop, we can stop it,' they said. It was shocking listening to Mum and to hear the kind of content I was not prepared for in the slightest: I struggled. Even on my wedding day, I was lumped with the emotional work. To humiliate her in front of this crowd of friends and cut her off mid-speech or to let her continue and deal with the fall out later? I just couldn't cut her off, even though it was my day and I felt so hurt, so violated. I worried about my queer friends in the room, of our shared histories, these stories. These shame-filled stories were their stories, too. On that phone call to Nate, weeks later, he said, 'Everyone was bawling, people have all tasted it.'

The misgendering seemed slight in comparison to the content of Mum's speech in which she declined to mention Merryn, or the reason we had all gathered on a large property in the Hunter Valley – the idea of marriage, our relation-ship, making a life together. The omission was heartbreaking. Someone slipped a drink into my hand. Mum continued, touching on a positive anecdote about teenage me. 'Yeah, Erin, you're fucking amazing,' someone cheered, interrupt-ing Mum mid-speech. Immediately, more and more people began chanting my name, clapping and cheering, holding me. Stomping their feet. Everyone began to clap in rhythm, still cheering, chanting my name and one by one, people rose, clapping, making noise, drowning out what was left of Mum's speech in a standing ovation. Holding her dignity.

The room roared.

When I think back to the wedding day, this moment is unforgettable. The ways queers love and care for one another is something we know well. The organising that goes into caring for community is historical and universal because structures and systems and families let us down and we create families of our own from the people we choose because they are there, without judgement or shame, to listen. If someone has no money, someone else organises a fundraiser. When my friend's mother died suddenly, a colour-coded roster of food-making was set up, and people dropped off soups and curries on the porch for an entire family. I have learnt about love as an action from the queer community I have found, and to feel this love at such a profound moment of immediate distress is something I will never forget. Look at how you are loved, Merryn whispered in my ear. My eyes filled with tears. I had never felt so moved by anything and the room was generously offered a temporary euphoria. This remarkable gesture of queer solidarity, queer joy, put us back on track, to reclaim the rest of that night. It was not ruined and we would not let this ruin it.

On a bench by the Cooks River, seven weeks after the wedding, Mum was dumbfounded when I explained how hurt I was, that her misgendering me the whole time felt painful and purposeful. I asked her why, what happened. The 'shes' were not intentional, apparently. She claimed to have not even written that word down on her palm cards. Later, on reflection, it was hard to believe it to be true, that it was possible to read what is not in front of your eyes. 'Why did you feel you needed to retell all of my trauma, Mum?' She saw her speech as telling my friends the 'truth', the story she thinks perhaps I have not myself told or retold many times over. Little does she know how queers are trauma bonded. She was trying, at least in her mind, to describe the rocky, messy, branch-stacked, bogged and muddy road I trod to the clearing in which I finally found myself, this crystalline, resilient, solid, me.

For her, the content was not so strange. Apparently, she was getting to the point – my relationship, my current life – when she was drowned out in purgative queer joy. I asked her more questions, about whether she saw me. She told me that she had 'always seen me' – that her seeing was always filled with love. I could feel her confusing but deep love there on the bench by the river and I knew it, I knew her love. I had come to meet her because the wedding left me so aghast that I doubted it momentarily. I also felt, profoundly, her rich love's limitations. I asked, then, about her interruption of the ceremony and she did not hold back her judgement, simply handed it over, as if talking about flavoured ice cream, as if it were not fucked-up at all to say, 'I thought that bit was a wank.'

I pieced things together, slowly, as best as I could. Mum saw the event as over the top, as ostentatious (we got married under a tree and danced on Astroturf), as theatrical – and somewhere in there, that spectacle was painful for her. She had lived in the shadows of her sisters, she was the one who described herself as 'always waiting' for things to happen. Who rarely went on holidays, who didn't allow herself the luxury of catching a taxi, who gave all her money away to those less fortunate. And here we were, these absolute wankers who had allowed ourselves all this space to stand up in, to be loved and be seen.

Mum is a real character. I have often spoken of her like this. She is full of gusto and charisma and weird idiosyncrasy. She is full of care and love and contradiction. I realised sitting next to her, finally, that she is also kind of mad. The author Deborah Levy's words came to me after I decided to drop the rope with Mum, to finally give up the consistent tug of war to be truly understood. I no longer, at thirty-eight, really needed her understanding in the way I needed it when I was less robust inside.

> Perhaps a character is someone who is not quite herself.
> I think that is what is meant when someone in life is
> described as being 'a bit of a character'.[36]

Mum slipped a delicately wrapped book about the writing life into my hand. I had already read it but she had ordered it from her local bookshop. The 'Spectrum' review was neatly cut out, placed on card and laminated and tucked inside like a bookmark. On the back, a loving handwritten note to me that included a quote from the review:

> Dear Erin,
> I pretty much agree that '. . . too often writers and literature
> are dismissed as mere icing on the cake of culture, as apart
> from an intrinsic part of it'. All my best to you Erin to
> provide more 'icing on the cake'. Love, Mum.

Vicki, mortified after Mum's speech, went up to Dad. 'You have to do something, the misgendering is not okay.' 'I will,' he said to her, 'I've got this.' Vicki came over to report that Dad believed he could bring us back. While he tried, Dad's entire speech, which in his tradition as a school-teacher-cum-poet he gave in verse, was also obsessed with gender. He spoke of himself as not being very woke, reflecting on a sort of 'before and after' experience of me, again, fixated on gender in a way fit for a therapy room, not a hundred of my favourite people. He talked about my 'testosterone-fuelled moustache' and the community I had found who loved me. I appreciated his efforts, though it was still humiliating for me, as if in his speech-giving process, he was trying to convince himself of my humanity. Nobody else at my wedding needed this proved to them.

He took time, at the wedding, to explain his affront, as an educator of the English language, at my request for a pronoun change. For him, this was a transgressive misuse of the plural 'they'. The room died again, I heard a few boos, people irate at his dismissal of their pronoun choice, so often the best of what is on offer from the coloniser's English.

Aboriginal languages do not have gendered pronouns. Claire G. Coleman, acclaimed Noongar writer, notes that this is not part of Aboriginal culture:

In the Noongar language – my ancestral tongue from the south coast of Western Australia – the word 'baal' means he, she, they or it; essentially it has the same meaning as the singular 'they' in English, yet it is broader, as it is also used to refer to the inanimate. The same word in Warlpiri, spoken mostly in a remote Western Desert community, is 'nyanungu'. I will keep searching for an Aboriginal language with gendered third-person pronouns, but I don't expect to find one.[37]

Dad's one-page Word document with the alliterative title, in response to my post-wedding email, was also written in verse. For the first time in a long time, he seemed to be aligning himself with Mum, upset on her behalf at my email, in which I expressed more disappointment in her than him. His poem dripped in misogyny and transphobia. It was reactive and rejecting and cruel. Its 236 words, fuelled by a rage and a hatred so deep that all I could do was weep in the middle of my workday supporting people whose parents often disown them for being trans and queer and different and for shimmering authentically. At thirty-eight, being rejected by family was not something I had anticipated. I had thought I was just getting married. For so long I'd been looking forward to the moment in which my worlds would finally meet.

Dad could not speak on behalf of himself in his strange stanza, though he told me that Mum had lost a 'daughter in more ways than one'. He described my friends as my 'coterie of acolytes' and considered the wedding to be my 'deification as some sort of queer Messiah'. He encouraged me to accept the challenge as a modifying minority user of the English language, to abandon my 'lazy word-washing parasitism' and develop a new language to explain myself.

In reading his response, I now understood, deeply, Dad's not-looking. I was making room for myself, in language and in space. A small word shift that, while not quite right, was all I had to be closer-to. Asking this was as if I was asking for the world. I chose to make an entire day all about me and my partner. A day to be as authentic and as strange as we wished. Maybe for Dad, this was too much. I wasn't a queer messiah; I was just me at my wedding being loved by my friends and wearing some fancy clothes. And for reasons maybe I will never know, but which I can only hypothesise, he felt big feelings about it. Big feelings that he turned inside out, refused to touch like a shit-stained jumper, and shot back at me through the internet in the form of venomous micro poetry.

Dad seemed contemptuous of my pain, as if giving something to queer people was taking something from him, that he was somehow disenfranchised if I took up more room. The way he spoke about me, about my friends; telling us all to 'toughen up, sweetlings' – as if we were pieces of shit. That we needed to get used to people making errors, of using language that harms us, because we were a minority. We needed to stop being wussy and make space for being hurt, intentionally or unintentionally. I held my rage, since, like his, it was reactive. Instead, I just sat down and held myself warmly. Merryn and I watched a lot of *Love Island UK*. We queers are as hard as nails, the world having long served us the conditions in which we always have to toughen up.

I did a lot of screenshotting of memes and Instagram stories that helped me in the weeks after the wedding, a period when I was experiencing such a jarring range of emotions. There was one about cis grief being something one should process with a therapist and absolutely never with one's trans kid and I lol'd because it was at least one hundred times worse when cis grief is processed in front of more than a hundred of your closest (mostly queer) friends at your own wedding.

I was more in love than ever and I was trying to wade through the shocking grief of what had happened with my family. I needed validation and affirmation that what happened was actually brutal. Friends texted me to see if I was okay and when, after the honeymoon, my friend Panda, one of the first to stand up at the wedding, delivered me a deconstructed and delicious pho with a step-by-step guide on how to assemble it, it was recognition that something profoundly painful had happened that day. I ate it in the sunshine on the couch outside on the porch and was halfway through when I got the call from my editor, who had phoned to let me know they wanted to publish this collection and to hurry up and write the story you are reading now.

The weeks following became more complex and grief-riddled as I processed the gravity of Dad's email, the final lines I read as advising me I was no longer welcome in the family home. It was an outright rejection I didn't see coming, with words so scathing I almost couldn't bear to open it and reread it in the writing of this essay.

My friend Archie, also a prolific reader, came up with the goods on Instagram, reposting a quote from one of my all-time favourite books, James Baldwin's *Giovanni's Room*:

There are so many ways of being despicable it quite makes one's head spin. But the way to be really despicable is to be contemptuous of other people's pain.[38]

I had been reading a lot, doing a lot of walking, podcast-listening, exercise-bike riding and taking myself to the ocean. I wanted to be free of the grief but it was hovering about like a seagull on a chip. 'You'll know what to do,' said my therapist. 'There is no rush, for these feelings will not kill you.' I say this to my clients, too, and when they ride the wave and emerge from under it, we acknowledge that we can bear the difficult things.

I thought about how queers ask for so little – a sliver of space, a small linguistic gesture, a few laws to protect us from hate crimes, a bathroom to take a shit in peace – somehow it is too much: it takes something away from those who have everything they need, it's a threat to their power or touches on a vulnerability. No. No. No. You may not have those small graces, who on earth do you think you are? We will fight very hard for you to not have those small things, even though we lose nothing by extending these accommodations to you. This is the kind of situation we live in; where anti-trans and anti-abortion legislation is mostly being fought for by people whose day-to-day life will look no different if what little protections we have are repealed. It feels painful to imagine the inner lives of those so dedicated to obliterating the quality of life of other people.

It is a big deal, to step towards something more authentically yourself, especially when you have played a particular role in your family. I knew I'd been staying small, out of my need for approval. Conflict in family systems can lead to chaos, especially for ones with problems, because they resist change. Business as usual is safe and comfortable. The person's wish to change is deeply threatening to the family system and the family will often attack the individual trying to flip the script.[39] In reading more about the Mother Wound and how patriarchy also fucks with men in families, I thought about my dad. His letter pathologising and attacking was his own attempt to maintain some family equilibrium. His message was clear:

> Your unwillingness to continue in the family system in your established role indicates that there is something deeply wrong with you.[40]

As Webster notes, 'this shame-based narrative abdicates [. . .] other family members from having to honestly examine their own behaviour and take responsibility'.[41] She reminds us that we cannot save our families, we can only save ourselves and people who go this far, resisting at all costs, their own stuff. Sometimes, ostracising their own child is a length people will go to remain in denial. This unconscious projection to resist change happens so often in conflict and, as personal as it feels, it's not personal at all, it's simply what happens when people have done nothing to explore their own inner life and are confronted with 'their own disowned pain through a catalysing event'.[42]

The first lines of the Mary Oliver poem Nate read at the ceremony go like this:

Everything that was broken has forgotten its brokenness.
I live now in a sky-house, through every window, the sun.[43]

Before the Word document, before the honeymoon, in which we spent time with chosen family by the beach and had conversations with friends from faraway, was the rest of the wedding. You might be reasonably convinced, after reading this far, that it sunk like a sack of potatoes. But you would be wrong. As Oliver prophesised, the brokenness was forgotten. It was as if the standing ovation, the exquisite moment of queer solidarity, had revived us from the brink of death – a breath so powerful that every person was elevated, infused with the courage to bring it back.

When Dad had finished with the mic, a scrum of guests put their heads together with mine and Merryn's. 'What next?' we asked one another. Vicki ushered people outside onto the Astroturf, as if the room needed to be emptied for a psychic deep clean. I grabbed a Scotch served in a thin plastic tumbler and sat silently for a minute. I could see my mum, across from me, sobbing at the middle table – in her black and teal dress, with her long, black gloves, alone among a sea of people. The kind of distress I used to believe I had caused, that I needed to fix. Outside under a sky filled with stars, Merryn's mum and dad got up to speak, welcoming me into a family where I had already found a home, reminding us of the enormity of what we had chosen to do together. The crowd gathered around them and then our best people got up and told equally embarrassing and loving stories of our friendships, their observations on love and connection.

In the weeks leading up to the wedding, we'd received a flurry of packages from the internet. One was my veil from Etsy. Twenty-five bucks. It lives in my sock drawer now but really needs to go. One night I got home and Merryn was slithering into a long-sleeved, sparkly silver sequined dress, short and hot and flattering. Next to it was a package from which I pulled out a similar shaped garment, though instead of sparkles it was covered in a white faux fuzz. Our wedding day costume change had arrived. Once a never nude, afraid of many things, including my own nakedness, I had moved towards a greater appreciation of my body. For how it kept me alive, how it carried me through the world. I was excited to dress like a slutty polar bear at our mid-winter wedding. I took the dress Merryn didn't want and because we don't have a full-sized mirror in the tiny periwinkle blue cottage, we took turns to stand on the small Ikea step ladder in the bathroom, contorting to avoid hitting our head on the ceiling to get a solid look in the mirrored cabinet above our broken sink.

Once the speeches were over, our friend Casper took over as DJ and people danced hard with a palpable jubilance. The restorative joy that had been sparked rippled through people's bodies and stuck there. Merryn and I disappeared into the house to breathe. Alone together, we were elated, exuberant and stunned. Peeling off our layers like wetsuits, we placed them gently in our suitcase on the floor. We also packed into it some of the night which we would open and take out some other time.

Stepping into our cheap frills, into the kind of outfit we'd have worn to that party in which our love began in a gutter in Faversham Street, Marrickville, high on MDMA, we clicked into a new gear. I put on the socks with eggplant emojis all over them and my Blundstones and kept the crown of pearls on my head. Merryn's cowboy boots stayed on and we rejoined our friends and danced and danced and I don't know how but my parents' words did not echo in my ears. I did not feel the pain of that. All we could do was smile and dance and hold close the raging freaks celebrating us with all our love and adoration.

Michael White was an Australian social worker who developed the therapeutic model Narrative Therapy. It's a politicised model, heavily influenced by philosopher Michel Foucault's observations on the operations of modern power, a kind of power that over the last few centuries has displaced previously coercive modes of traditional power and has become the main system in achieving social control:

> This is a power that recruits people's active participation in the fashioning of their own lives, their relationships, and their identities, according to the constructed norms of culture – we are both a consequence of this power and a vehicle for it [. . .] It is a power that is everywhere to be perceived in its local operations, in our intimate lives and relationships. Foucault sought to illustrate the many ways that we live our lives on the inside of the web of power relations of this system of modern power, and to draw attention to the extent to which we have become its unwitting instruments.[44]

White writes a lot about the concept of personal failure – which is why people go to therapy – this sense that they have failed life in some way. This modern phenomenon of personal failure is

> connected to 'the rise of a distinctly modern version of power that establishes the effective system of social control through what can be referred to as "normalising judgement".'[45] Whereas traditional systems of power operate through moral judgement, modern systems of power encourage people to police themselves and each other's lives against a rigid set of socially constructed norms.[46]

Much of the technology of modern power was developed by the professional disciplines, such as medicine and psychiatry, but has come to shape modes of living. When thinking about this idea of failure, White makes clear that what is happening is that people are increasingly being asked to meet a range of idealised norms for personhood that are replicated and idealised in culture and when they can't meet them, end up with feelings of failure and otherness, worthlessness, inadequacy and so on. People are working so hard in life to live up to these norms that attract social capital, and they have been internalised so much that many of us believe achieving them is what amounts to being a good person.[47]

Staying in line within this system is, then, to avoid social snubbing (e.g. in performing gender in the ways that have been culturally fashioned as 'normal' – i.e. not trans). Those who fail to meet the norms set up by modern power find themselves policed by others (e.g. discrimination, actual violence and abuse in the form of racism, transphobia or homophobia, ableism, etc), believing themselves failures in some way or another (body not skinny enough, not buff enough, hot enough, productive enough, feminine enough, heterosexual enough, masculine enough, too weak, too effeminate, too fat, too crazy, etc). Some unwittingly then participate in their own self-policing, exiling parts of themselves that do not meet these norms in order to remain safe in a culture that privileges and rewards certain kinds of identity and self-expression.

For White, Foucault's ideas, while morbidly depressing, opened up new ways of thinking about resistance. Where there is power, there is resistance, and if modern power requires people's active participation to sustain itself, then it is incredibly fragile because it makes room for people to subvert its operation. It is then, White contends, in challenging the 'dispositions and habits that are fashioned by modern power, people can play a part in denying this power its conditions of possibility'.[48] The aim, at least in a therapy space, is to help people develop an awareness of modern power in order to recognise their desperate desire to reach the unreachable, and their idea of personal 'failure' could be seen, from another angle, as a refusal to play into the reproduction of norms that actually aren't serving them, and might even be obscuring their deeper authenticity.

> It is in this sense that we might find, in the shadows of failure, other knowledges of life and practices of living that do not so directly reproduce the cherished norms of the contemporary world.[49]

Queers have always been failing the test, if the test is the internalising of socially constructed norms about what it means to be an authentic and worthwhile person in society. Mostly everyone at the wedding had some experience of not shoring up the standards of gender and sexuality that the machinations of modern power overwhelmingly demands and socially rewards. After years of self-policing and exposure to normative judgement, we had recognised that our refusal to meet the standards of living set by families and culture and the larger structures of life was an identity project that was actually fulfilling, rich and worth pursuing. In living in an identity that society continues to affirm is not what is required of us, that our position is unfavourable, we have fashioned communities of care and safety, because being openly queer is to refuse to engage in the reproductive norms that modern power and current culture demand. To refuse, still sadly means people are met with steely opposition, an unconscious clinging for dear life to the norms we believe are the definers of a good life. In my case it is to be met with the artillery fire of my mum's 'hers' and 'shes' and Dad's poetic brevity, with its reminder of my place in the shadows.

At the wedding, these norms were flipped, if only for the day. The majority of people there were queers and freaks. On reflection, even though my parents failed their test to honour and see me as I needed them to, our crowd of people, full of those so often policed socially and culturally, did not do the same to them; they did not fall into a need to police my parents, didn't tell them to leave, didn't cut them off, tell them they did not belong. No, they provided a kind alternative, one that held space for dignity in pain and that acknowledged that structures and ideas are intellectual cages, from which love is a way out. It was almost a utopian space, the wedding, because queer people don't often hold or occupy spaces where power is ours. The standing ovation, the energetic moving of Mum mid-speech offstage was the opposite of the social policing that modern power produces, which says something about the communities and people and ways of doing life we tend to judge.

I had really hoped the wedding would see the blending of my worlds, for Mum and Dad to see into this life of mine, where normalising judgement was something people had spent time attempting to unpick and unpack. I was excited about it finally happening but sadly, they enacted their own resistance. I get it; there is safety and value and social reward in doing this, but it was and remains one of the most heartbreaking moments of my life. There are, as always, consequences for displaying authenticity in a world that remains regressive – and one of the risks is to be met with rejection.

Today, as I finish this final chapter it is Father's Day. I have not spoken to my dad in the two and a half months since the wedding. I have not replied to his email, in which he asked me to find my humility in order to be let back in. Thing is, I do not need to be let back in. I no longer need my parents' understanding, or to be known in the ways I once needed because I can do this for my adult self. While it's no longer a need, I would, however, love it to be something that is on offer to me, and that my vulnerability will one day be understood as the gift it is. Modern power dynamics, and the normative ideas that keep us disconnected and treating each other contemptuously leave us all ideologically caged, having to reproduce and toe the manufactured line of what it means to be a person. I like living in the expansive shadow of failure, and have always lived here. I want for Mum and Dad to see that it's a cage, but that the door's always been open, waiting for them to find their wings, and fly out.

Afterword
December 2022

I had top surgery a week ago. In medical terms, a double mastectomy. When I was giving informed consent for the procedure a minute before I wandered into the operating theatre with my TED stockings and my hair net and my forehead covered in electrode pads, they asked me what I was having done. To which I replied, without hesitation: 'I'm having my titties chopped off.' We all laughed and then they lopped them right off.

I'm writing this afterword in my lounge room surrounded by the fluff from a toy crocodile Remy has destroyed because she knows some of the attention is on me. The edits to this book came back to me on the Friday, the day I returned home from hospital in my oversized button-up, a pillow strapped to my chest in the car. I was in some pain initially, which has been mostly replaced by a more profound feeling of temporary incapacity and a desire to take good care of myself. I'm spending a lot of time in deep gratitude for both the body's incredible capacity to heal itself and for how lucky I am to have the privilege to access this kind of medical affirmation that allows people like me to inch towards a body that feels more aligned. I am manoeuvring around the house like a wounded bird, trying not to topple over every time I stand up. Being looked after is a new experience for me, always the carer, the one who rescues. Merryn has showered me a few times this week and for a minute there, I needed help getting my undies on.

I returned home to boxes of fancy premade meals delivered to my doorstep by kind friends, care packages full of books and chockies and homemade curries, flowers and impromptu visits. People came over for tea and took our Remy for a walk. I have been loved hard and by so many. It seems only fitting that this is the story, my own moving towards an authentic embodying of self, that has become possible, in part and process, from the writing of the stories in this collection.

My journey to publishing a book has been the marriage of great luck, incredible opportunity and persistence. Getting to this place also owes itself to my partner, Merryn, who, four years ago on my birthday, gifted me a four-week night-school writing class where I penned a short story about the pool next door to the apartment we would one day share. I had not written anything creative since I was an assistant editor of a student rag in the early aughts except for what I believed to be some of the most narratively rich reports on my geriatric community clients. A goal of mine, always, was to use words and writing in my job to elevate the parts of marginalised people's lives that are often unseen. I don't know if I'd have taken myself to that class without the encouragement.

I have been writing these stories, in my head, for years. I had often been unsure exactly how to merge all the things that mattered to me, especially when it came to justice-doing and systemic oppression and my curiosity about people's lives. I began to pen a few pieces, unsure where they would find homes, after I felt profoundly moved reading the work of authors Fiona Wright, Alexander Chee and Olivia Laing. Part of me was just so inspired to write, another part wanted to inspire this kind of feeling, somewhat outside language, in other people. For someone who finds it very hard to sit still, slowly and surely coming to an understanding that I have been blessed with a neurodivergent brain, reading these kinds of books is one of my life's deepest pleasures. All this to say, I applied to Penguin Random House Australia's Write It fellowship in 2021 on a whim. I sent in every word (7000) I had ever written. I made it to a shortlist and then, remarkably, made it to a list of four fellow fellows and spent a year just writing. I did the writing in between work and changing jobs and in fits and spurts on my days off. I tried to create a writing routine, but mostly stories just poured out of me when they were ready. Sometimes in a day or two. Having such a structured opportunity and empowered by the initial validation that my writing was worth putting energy into helped me tap away on this project. Over the year, I just wrote the things that mattered to me. Somehow, the manuscript I produced in that time, this loose collection of stories, had threads tight enough to see them weaved together into a publishable collection.

Initially, I had no real intention of writing a memoir. I was writing about outsiders whose lives were affected by injustice, trauma, hardship, rejection and otherness. I soon realised that these were structures that affected me and that their stories echoed my own. And so, I allowed myself to edge into the frame.

Writing myself into these stories, turning the curiosity inwards, has been one of the most healing aspects of writing this book. I am grateful to this book, for all that it has taught me about myself, especially what is possible for my life. I have grown into myself in part due to the deep reflection and compassion this project has required of me.

Even looking back on the pieces today, I can see my own growing-into. In the first story I ever wrote, 'Daughters', which became the prologue to this collection, I had still not learnt to gender myself in a way that felt right and allowed me to laugh off belittling comments. I accepted things, words, language I know I will no longer tolerate.

It is wild to think that, just four years after taking that writing class, I have published a book. I read and listen to people's tumultuous publishing journeys, those of crushing rejection, the ongoing waiting and searching for the right home for stories busting to be told. The arbitrary nature of it all and the stuff we know too well, that the mechanics of a for-profit system are at work in the world of books, too. My path to publishing, to 'becoming' a writer, has been unusually smooth. My actual life, less smooth. The process of becoming an embodied, kind, authentic version of myself might be more akin to many people's writing journey – one that has been fraught with failure and rejection. And, like the process of many writers, one that has needed constant rewriting, reflection and revision.

I have had some anxiety about publishing this collection and that anxiety, I know, is communication from the young part of me, an inner protector, that so often contorted itself into smaller shapes to fit in, to be liked, to avoid hurting people. That didn't say or do things to ensure other people were not made uncomfortable. It's a part that worries about how my parents will feel on reading the pieces about our family, about some of the hard things that have happened lately. I have daily conversations with this inner child and I remind them that we can cope when people are upset, that people can manage their own hard feelings – for this is no longer a job we have to keep doing. I know that my parents can manage, and they will survive whatever feelings might arise from reading my book.

My parents, since the wedding, have taken significant steps to repair the damage and this has been something I have welcomed. On my return from hospital, Mum left George Saunders's new short story collection, (suitably titled *Liberation Day*) on the front porch, alongside a hand-picked flower from her garden. My dad, two days before my surgery, wrote me a sincere and heartfelt apology for his painful email and wished me well for the procedure, indicating a desire to work towards something better between us. I have begun to see new readings of our relationship flickering into being and am discovering that, like Eve Kosofsky Sedgwick noted in her essay, maybe our future can be different from the present. Maybe less paranoid and more open.

On receipt of these offerings of repair, the old protective impulse from years ago piped up inside me in the familiar form of feeling hesitant to tell the stories in the way you have just read them.

But knowing I am a fully-fledged, reflective, loveable adult, no longer small and vulnerable, I have changed nothing, because this is what happened and these stories are mine. I also know that stories are not fixed, and we each have our own and they are continually being written.

Notes

1 Vikki A. Reynolds, 'Resisting burnout with justice-doing', *The International Journal of Narrative Therapy and Community Work*, vol. 2011, no. 4 pp. 36–7.

2 Frank Anderson, two-day workshop: Clinical Applications of Internal Family Systems.

3 Fiona Wright, *The World Was Whole*, Giramondo Publishing, Artarmon, 2018, p. 146.

4 Ibid.

5 Ibid.

6 Ibid, p. 148.

7 Ibid, p. 150.

8 Ibid, p. 157.

9 Ibid, p. 158.

10 Annie Dillard, *The Writing Life*, Harper Perennial, New York, 1989, p. 32.

11 Ibid.

12 Fiona Wright, *The World Was Whole*, Giramondo Publishing, Artarmon, 2018, p. 161.

13 Angela Duckworth quoted in Cave, Damien, *Into the Rip: How the Australian Way of Risk Made My Family Stronger, Happier . . . and Less American*, Scribner, Sydney, 2021, p. 193.

14 Ibid.

15 Ibid.

16 Cave, Damien, *Into the Rip: How the Australian Way of Risk Made My Family Stronger, Happier . . . and Less American*, Scribner, Sydney, 2021, p. 193.

Notes

17   Vikki A. Reynolds, 'Resisting burnout with justice-doing', *The International Journal of Narrative Therapy and Community Work*, vol. 2011, no. 4, p. 36.

18   Maggie Nelson and Olivia Laing: The Argonauts, London Review Bookshop, 2016, https://www.youtube.com/watch?v=s-Yxhc2nNxo&t=2762s

19   Olivia Laing on Everybody with Maggie Nelson, The Center for Fiction, 2021, https://www.youtube.com/watch?v=veQkCdXVqRw&t=2s

20   Eve Kosofsky Sedgwick, Michèle Aina Barale, Johnathan Goldberg, Michael Moon, *Touching Feeling: Affect, Pedagogy, Performativity*, Duke University Press, Durham, 2003.

21   Maggie Nelson and Olivia Laing: The Argonauts, London Review Bookshop, 2016, https://www.youtube.com/watch?v=s-Yxhc2nNxo&t=2751s

22   Olivia Laing, *Funny Weather: Art in an Emergency*, Picador, London, 2020, p. 4.

23   Olivia Laing, *Everybody: A Book About Freedom,* Picador, London, 2021, p. 284.

24   Maggie Nelson, *The Argonauts*, Text, Melbourne, 2015, p. 10.

25   Olivia Laing, *Everybody: A Book About Freedom*, Picador, London, 2021, p. 284.

26   Maggie Nelson, *The Argonauts*, Text, Melbourne, 2015, p. 9.

27   Eve Kosofsky Sedgwick, 'Paranoid Reading, Reparative Reading; or, You're So Paranoid You Probably Think This Introduction is About You' in Eve Kosofsky Sedgwick, Michèle Aina Barale, Johnathan Goldberg, Michael Moon, *Touching Feeling: Affect, Pedagogy, Performativity*, Duke University Press, Durham, 2003, p. 146.

28   Ibid.

29   Ibid p. 147.

30   Olivia Laing, *Funny Weather: Art in an Emergency*, Picador, London, 2020, p. 263.

31   Maggie Nelson, *The Argonauts*, Text, Melbourne, 2015, p. 3.

32   Bethany Webster, *Discovering the Inner Mother*, HarperCollins, New York, 2020, p. 6.

33   Ibid pp. 14–15.

34   Ibid pp. 18–19.

35   Ibid p. 18.

36   Deborah Levy, *Real Estate*, Penguin Books, London, 2021, p. 232.

Notes

37 Claire G. Coleman, Aboriginal Feminism and Gender, 9 April 2020, National Gallery of Victoria, https://www.ngv.vic.gov.au/essay/aboriginal-feminism-and-gender/

38 James Baldwin, *Giovanni's Room*, Penguin Classics, London, 2000, p. 56.

39 Bethany Webster, *Discovering the Inner Mother*, HarperCollins, New York, 2020, p. 150.

40 Ibid.

41 Ibid.

42 Ibid. p. 151.

43 Mary Oliver, *Felicity*, Penguin Books, London, 2015, p. 61.

44 Michael White, 'Addressing Personal Failure', *The International Journal of Narrative Therapy and Community Work*, vol. 2002, no. 3, p. 36.

45 (Foucault 1973, 1979, 1980) in ibid. p. 43.

46 Ibid.

47 Ibid.

48 Ibid. p. 36.

49 Ibid. p. 47.

Bibliography

Books

Cave, Damian, *Into the Rip: How the Australian Way of Risk Made My Family Stronger, Happier . . . and Less American*, Scribner, Sydney, 2021.

Dana, Deb, *The Polyvagal Theory in Therapy: Engaging the rhythm of regulation*, W.W. Norton & Company Inc, New York, 2018.

Dillard, Annie, *The Writing Life*, Harper Perennial, New York, 1990.

Laing, Olivia, *Funny Weather: Art in an Emergency*, Picador, London, 2020.

Laing, Olivia, *Everybody: A book about freedom*, Picador, London, 2021.

Nelson, Maggie, *The Argonauts*, Text, Melbourne, 2015.

Oliver, Mary, *Felicity*, Penguin Books, London, 2015.

Schwartz, Richard, *No Bad Parts*, Sounds True, Louisville, 2021.

Webster, Bethany, *Discovering the Inner Mother*, HarperCollins, New York, 2020.

Wright, Fiona, *The World Was Whole*, Giramondo, Artarmon, 2018.

Articles

Reynolds, Vikki A., 'Resisting burnout with justice-doing', *The International Journal of Narrative Therapy and Community Work*, vol. 2011, no. 4, pp. 27–45.

Sakellariou, Dikaios and Elana S. Rotarou, 'The effects of neoliberal policies on access to healthcare for people with disabilities', *International Journal for Equity in Health*, vol. 2017, no. 16, pp. 199–207.

White, Michael, 'Addressing Personal Failure', *The International Journal of Narrative Therapy and Community Work*, vol. 2022, no. 3, pp. 33–76.

Bibliography

Online

Maggie Nelson and Olivia Laing: The Argonauts, https://www.youtube.com/watch?v=s-Yxhc2nNxo&t=2762s

Olivia Laing on Everybody with Maggie Nelson, https://www.youtube.com/watch?v=veQkCdXVqRw&t=2s

Acknowledgements

This book was written on unceded Gadigal Land. I acknowledge that Aboriginal and Torres Strait Islander people are the traditional custodians of this stolen land and pay my respects to the long tradition of the land's first storytellers.

Firstly, I want to thank my partner, Merryn, whose enthusiastic and creative encouragement of my fledgling interest in writing was instrumental in inspiring this collection. Thank you for seeing me, for loving me and for leading me in the right direction. Your love has opened up so much space to dream and to write. I am grateful for all the ways you have supported me during the writing of this book, especially your fine eye during the last weeks of editing. I love you and the family we have made and the way we do life together. This book is for you, my love.

This collection emerged out of a year-long Write It Fellowship with Penguin Random House in 2021. Being shortlisted was cause for celebration on its own. Actually being awarded the mentorship was wild to me, and the reality that this has dovetailed into a collection that you hold in your beautiful hands remains an absolute, dizzying joy. The fellowship and the editorial mentoring that came with it gave my writing validation and me the encouragement and structure to keep writing. It is prizes and opportunities like these that make writers out of people like me.

Thank you to the team at Penguin Random House for their enthusiasm, kindness, expertise and support. I have learnt so much about the incredibly collaborative nature of publishing a book and am beyond grateful to every person that has gifted this book their expertise. Thank you to George Saad, who designed the stunning cover. You are so skilled at what you do. I am delighted.

Thank you, especially, to my editor and publisher Clive Hebard, who was also my mentor during the Write It Fellowship, for your time, energy and attention. Thank you for showing me how great editing can lift a story. Thank you for seeing the threads that weave through these pieces, for your humour and incredible skill. I'm thrilled we got to do this together from start to finish. I also love that we are equally enamoured with swimming.

Thank you to the people and places who first published my work, including versions of stories that ended up in this collection: *Kill Your Darlings*, *Enby Life*, *Bent Street* and Spineless Wonders.

Thank you to my queer community for growing me. I have been enriched, nourished and politicised by Sydney's queer community. It was here that I first found chosen family and a place for myself. It's also where I first felt unconditional acceptance. This book is for queers everywhere.

Acknowledgements

To old and new friends – my chosen family – who are too numerous to name but include especially Vicki, Kirthana, Brooke, Amy, Sangita, Sally, Teresa, Tonia, Zero, Casper, Mira, Claire, Alethea, Harry, Raquel and Jane, Panda and Becca, thank you for holding me so solidly in friendship.

Thank you to Tia and Bay for the double dates, rural getaways, endless board games and ease of friendship.

Thanks to the A Team – Nate McCarthy, Beth McNamara and Letty Funston. I treasure you all.

Thanks to Mel, who first gave me a copy of Fiona Wright's *The World Was Whole*, which, on reading, inspired me to pick up my pen. I'm not sure this book would exist without you. To Fiona Wright, whom I first accosted in true fan fashion, thank you for your early mentorship, your wise advice, and for generously sharing your knowledge with me.

To my early readers, especially Sarah Pisani, Archie, Mally, Ariana, Shannon, Leilani, Esther, Kathleen and Jill, and Stewart Kellie. Your generous feedback and engagement with the work was invaluable. Thank you.

Jaime, my long-distance bibliophile. Thank you for leading me to the books I needed to read and for your ecstatic response to the news of this collection.

Thank you to the SUCKERS. Diving into the ocean week in, week out with you all and taking more risks has been one of the most exhilarating experiences of my thirties.

To Karen, the first therapist I ever took myself to see, who helped me pick apart some of those early and limiting stories. You once asked me if I sometimes felt like I was just tolerating things in life, and suggested that perhaps there was more in life for me, if I wanted it. There really was!

To my current therapist, Rachel, thank you for pointing out my responsible part, helping me to get to know it and to begin shifting gears. Thank you also for being one of my first and most enthusiastic readers. Your support, unconditional acceptance and generosity is a gift.

Thank you to Maeve Marsden of Queerstories, who gave me the opportunity to perform my first-ever story, 'Daughters', in 2019, which became the accidental prologue to this collection.

Thank you to Kate, my social work supervisor, who helped ensure the ethics we are bound by remained robust and central to the pieces relating to my work.

Thank you to the social workers who changed my life and first mentored me in the community – Helen, Marsia, Carole, Nina and Sophie. Your fierce advocacy, practice wisdom and creativity was and remains inspiring to me. I treasure our time in that cramped Canterbury office. I hope that this book speaks to the unseen and invaluable work of social workers everywhere.

To my family. Firstly, thank you to the Kellies: Stewart and Jill, Jed and Jess, Nick and Bianca, Ollie and Lucy – thank you for your thoroughly enthusiastic support of this project from day one. I'm so happy to call you family.

And finally, to my mum Antoinette, my dad John, my sister Claire and my Aunt G. Thank you for your support and your love. The stories that are about us are a tribute to love and its complexity, the nuanced nature of relationships and family and the messy structural contexts in which we all swim.

Acknowledgements

These are my perspectives, my reflections, and my intention in writing this collection has been to explore how experiences shape us and our stories. In so doing, I wanted to write the book I needed when I was younger. I hope you read this with the love, curiosity and compassion in which it was written. I love you.

Text Permissions

Discover a
new favourite